D0681491

CONFESSIONS OF
A SERIAL DIETER

'Kalli has demystified the process of living a healthy, fit and fulfilling life. People's lifestyles have changed, dramatically inducing associated health challenges. This book is a candid chronicle of surmounting weightloss challenges, lucidly illustrated through Kalli's own experiments and experiences. Life is indeed about choices and decisions and Kalli gracefully points us to some of the most important ones. This book will inspire anyone who is in the pursuit of change!'
Nita Ambani

'My weight has always been a battle. It's something that is very close to my heart. Being thin is about so much more than just your weight. For no matter how thin I get, inside I'll always be a fat girl. Only a fellow dieter can understand that.'
Sonam Kapoor

'Weight loss is not just about shedding kilos, it's an emotional journey. Dieticians don't get that, *Serial Dieter* does.'
Sonakshi Sinha

'Reading *Serial Dieter* was like reading my own life story. This is the first diet book that gives tips that may not be approved by dieticians but are real. Tried and tested. It takes one dieter to know another. And she is one helluva dieter. She has done 43 diets, I have done 40, so the coffee hamper for now goes to her.'
Karan Johar

CONFESSIONS OF A SERIAL DIETER

Secrets from 43 diets and workouts that took me from 100 to 60

Kalli Purie

HarperCollins *Publishers* India

a joint venture with

New Delhi

First published in India in 2012 by
HarperCollins *Publishers* India
a joint venture with
The India Today Group

Copyright © Kalli Purie 2012

ISBN: 978-93-5029-184-9

2 4 6 8 10 9 7 5 3 1

HarperCollins Publishers
A-53, Sector 57, Noida 201301, India
77-85 Fulham Palace Road, London W6 8JB, United Kingdom
Hazelton Lanes, 55 Avenue Road, Suite 2900, Toronto, Ontario M5R 3L2
and 1995 Markham Road, Scarborough, Ontario M1B 5M8, Canada
25 Ryde Road, Pymble, Sydney, NSW 2073, Australia
31 View Road, Glenfield, Auckland 10, New Zealand
10 East 53rd Street, New York NY 10022, USA

Design & illustrations by Kushal Grover

Typeset in Arno Pro 11/14
by Jojy Philip

Printed and bound at
Thomson Press (India) Ltd.

For the one who loved me the most when I loved myself the least

CONTENTS

WHY I CAN WRITE
THIS BOOK

Because I am no dietician or trainer. I am a serial
dieter. I have been there, done that diet. Rather,
43 of them. And survived to tell the tale.

WHY I AM QUALIFIED

I was born premature, a mere 2.5 kg. By the time I was one, I was overweight – and this is when my choice of food was limited to mashed apples and bananas. At the age of four, I was capable of complicated barters with my friends at pre-school, which left them with my bottle filled with good old tap water and me with their chocolate truffle pastries. At four, I was on my first diet. After that there was no looking back. Since then I have done over forty diet and workout programmes, some of them twice over.

I confess that I am a serial dieter.

I have been 55 kg and 104 kg. And that, I would say, is a weighty list of qualifications.

I am no guru.

Thin doctors and fit dieticians can harp on about the healthy way to lose weight but they don't understand the mind, moods and miseries of a fat person. They have never been in that fat suit. They have not walked down that road. But because they meet and help so many people with the same problem they have some really good solutions and perspectives. Yet it's not the same. Dieticians and trainers can tell you what to do and help you do it. But they have not done it. I have.

If someone had told me all the things I've learnt the hard way, maybe it wouldn't have taken me thirty years to get here. I learnt something from every diet, dietician, fat farm, trainer and exercise programme, and it was a slow process. My understanding has evolved over millions of calories and is almost as advanced as Darwin's theory of the survival of the fittest. The death of the fattest. By sharing my story, I hope I can help you reach your goal faster. And maybe for all my good work, god will make me thin in my next life.

WHY I NEED TO WRITE THIS BOOK...

Now that I am (almost) the weight I have lost, my biggest fear is gaining it back.

This book is an insurance policy of sorts. But there are other reasons for writing it. I have reached a new weight nirvana. I feel I can look the weighing scale straight in the eye. I want to share some of the things I have learnt. It's to keep me on the right track but it is also to help others get on the right track.

...AND WHY YOU NEED TO READ IT

Thin people lie

You think thin people are just thin. You ask someone, 'You look wonderful – what are you doing?' She says, 'Oh, nothing. Just controlling my diet and going to the gym.' Sounds familiar? You keep meeting these PYTs and they look slimmer each time. Then one day you turn up at the dietician's and there she is. Pants down, tummy out, having the fat massaged out of her. Why don't people who lose weight share their secrets? Maybe it's a fear that others will become thin too and they will lose their calorie advantage. Or they feel ashamed that they need help to lose weight.

'I'm naturally thin'

This is a lie. Anyone who is thin after thirty works at it. They are doing *something*. I have a friend who is 5'3" and weighs 42 kg. She is really slim. But if she eats two slices of superthin oven-roasted pizza she frets about it for three days and compensates for another three with green tea and salad.

I am telling you, anybody who looks good looks that way because they are doing something about it.

Yes, metabolic rates matter, but only till you're thirty. I have seen thin people who did nothing to stay fit all their life cross thirty and either start to get heavy around the middle or just get careful. They automatically skip dessert, take the stairs, and talk more than they eat at dinner parties.

Of course, some people have a faster metabolic rate and tend not to put on weight. But if you eat without control and don't exercise, you will put on weight no matter how fast your metabolic rate. You might be blessed but the blessing doesn't last long without gratitude.

Weight is a sensitive topic

Most fat people are really bothered by their weight. It affects their very being. When I was fat, I could never be in any conversation that related to weight. I would feel the urgent need to hide, leave or change the topic immediately. My weight was an embarrassment to me. It's pretty hard to tell a gathering, 'Yes, I weigh 100 kg.' Most people don't want to face it. They would rather hide behind their huge kaftans.

I hated being fat. I was not cute. And it was not funny. The jokes, the jibes, they hurt. And telling us, 'Hey, you have really put on weight,' does not help. (Yes, thank you, how considerate of you to have noticed.)

But if nobody notices, you continue down the same path of self-delusion. This puts friends and family in a tough spot. Do they/should they/can they tell you? Friends and family do, but only up to a point.

The vicious circle

Being fat is a vicious circle. You put on weight. You look not so good. Nothing fits. You are down and out. You eat some chocolate.

You feel good. You eat some more. Put on more weight. Now you are looking worse and feeling worse and need more chocolate. And so it goes. Losing weight has its own circle. The Virtuous Circle. You lose weight. You wear beautiful clothes. You go out. Everybody tells you you look great. You feel great. You skip the starters. You drink champagne. You work out harder. You drop another size. You look fantastic. And so it goes.

Fat is not beautiful

Many people believe that being thin or wanting to be thin is falling for the marketing ploy spun by the big beauty and diet multinationals who have created unrealistic body ideals to keep themselves in business. It isn't. Being fit is how we are designed to be. It's not about being model skinny, it's about being your ideal weight and that is not 20 kg over the average for your height. Drop the illusion. Fat is not beautiful.

I don't have the time but I have the weight

There is no such thing as 'I don't have the time to exercise'. Time is what we make of it. As my wise mother says, 'We always make time for what we really want to do.' I buy that 100 per cent. Those who exercise also have only twenty-four hours in the day. You have to choose your priorities and follow them, come what may. And exercise has to be top of the list.

I work full time

Just because you work full time does not give you the licence to eat full time. Unhealthy eating and hard work are not connected. Late nights at the office ordering in pizza and working lunches with mayo-loaded sandwiches is detrimental to any healthy plan. There is no easy way around this. You simply have to be committed to it. Carry your own tiffin, choose the unpopular healthy meal. It might be a little awkward at first but you'll get used to it.

Your other excuses are invalid too

I want to tell you that the reasons you are giving yourself not to lose weight are all invalid.

I have a great personality. She is thin but insipid.
But think how much more fantastic you will be if you are thinner and have a great personality.

She is only thin because her husband thinks of her as a trophy wife. Mine loves me the way I am.
Yes, but how much more will he love you when you are looking super hot.

She has a hot body. But look at her nose. At least I have a nice face.
A nice face doesn't make you healthy and a hot body complements a pretty face very well.

She lost her personality when she lost her weight.
Fat people don't have better personalities. They are not bubblier or happier. It's a front. And you can be all those things and also be thin. The two are not related.

She has lost so much weight, her face has shrunk. At least I don't have any wrinkles.
Wrinkles and fat are not really connected, although I agree that beyond a certain amount of weight loss the face can look shrunken and lined. This is a tough choice. Thin and wrinkly vs fat and smooth. I think I choose cheekbones.

Losing weight is not just about looking good

Yes, the clothes fit better. (Hell! You can buy clothes from a *shop*. They don't have to be custom-made kurtis from the garage tailor aunty.) But losing weight is not just about looking good. That's only part of it. You feel good because everything fits better, not just your clothes.

We are social beings. We want others to like what they see. Fat people often create a negative first impression. Shallow society? Yes, but also animal instinct. It's the basic law of our existence. We are naturally attracted to those specimens that are fit and healthy. Being fat is unhealthy. You double the strain on your heart, lungs, knees. You are not a top specimen.

Fit people are pre-judged positively. Knowing that others like what they see when they look at you is a great confidence booster. You are not watching every word you say to ensure a positive impression because you have already made it. This is very liberating.

Look the part

If you don't look the part, they won't let you do the part. You can spend your life fighting this and say that it's 'boxy' and everyone is unique. But just like a model needs to be tall and thin because his or her job is to showcase clothes, as a member of any team, you need to be in control. A fat person, by definition, does not have control over

In 1998, at an investors' forum in New York, an analyst cheekily asked Reliance's Anil Ambani how he could be trusted to manage a huge business when he obviously couldn't take care of his own health. Ambani weighed in at over 100 kg then; today, he is 62 kg.

his desires. This does not mean that fat people can't lead companies or get promotions, it just means they have to work that much harder to prove that they can.

Slotting over slothing

'I can't meet you for coffee in the evening because I am going to the bank in the morning.' When I was fat, I could do only one thing in a day. I either went for a doctor's appointment or had coffee with a friend or went shopping. I could not do multiple things in a day. When you are overweight, everything is an effort except eating and sleeping.

Now my whole day is slotted. You end up doing so much more with your life when you are not carrying a fat person on your back. Life is limited, what you do with it is not. I want to juice out every minute. Before, I would curl up for hours under a warm razai and read a book with a bar of dark chocolate, every single day. I still love to curl up with a good book and a few squares of chocolate, but after a hectic day and as a way to unwind. Not as my activity for the day.

This was my average day in Jan 2007

(I was a full-time mom with two children in Delhi)

8.00 a.m. Wake up.

9.00 a.m. Drop kids to school.

9.30 a.m. Coffee and muffins with friends. Gossip.

12.15 p.m. School pick up.

1.00 p.m. Lunch. Often out, sometimes in. Always heavy. End with something sweet. (Sample lunch: yellow dal, white rice, sweet tomato chutney, fried bhindi, aloo jeera, chocolate)

2.00–4.30 p.m. Can't keep eyes open. Change into kaftan or PJs and sleep.

5.00 p.m. Playdate with kids at Nehru Park, involving snacks (popcorn, ice-cream, Gems). Lie around while kids run around.

7.00 p.m. More snacking and raiding (biscuits, aloo lachcha chips from the halwai shop).

7.30 p.m. Dead tired.

8.00 p.m. Complain about night plans because I had such a busy day.

8.30 p.m. Cancel plans. Change into PJs. Eat dinner (mountain of white rice with a heavy coconut fish curry). Vegetate in front of the TV while chomping down leftover chocolate.

Midnight. Bed.

Minimum activity. Maximum food. Boring, lazy, unfit, sort of happy and very fat.

This was my average day in Jan 2009

(Still a full-time mom with two children in Delhi)

7.00 a.m. Up with baby boy who has to go to the pot. Washing bottom before washing face!

7.30 a.m. Cuddle in bed with babies. Energizer.

8.00 a.m. Tea and papers.

9.00–11.00 a.m. Workout.

11.20 a.m. Shopping in Select Citywalk to check out latest sales and buy long-pending gifts. Plate of fruit for breakfast in the car.

1.00 p.m. School pick up.

1.45 p.m. Get the kids to change and supervise lunch. Lunch with friend at home. Friend eats rice and fish curry and dark chocolate-covered biscuits. I stick to cabbage soup* diet.

3.15 p.m. Park outing for kids and their friends. Walk and run with the children.

*The cabbage soup diet is essential compensation for all new year indulgences.

4.30 p.m. Kids go riding on ponies. I follow on foot.

5.30 p.m. Home.

6:00 p.m. Visit friend who just had a baby girl. Give long-pending gift. Have green tea. Send away the biscuits.

7.15 p.m. Home. Quality time with the children, bath, story, bed.

8.00 p.m. Shower and change.

8.20 p.m. Cabbage soup in the car.

8.30 p.m. Out with friends.

9.15 p.m. Dinner at a Vietnamese restaurant. Stirfry and raw salads. No to spring rolls. No to rice. No to noodles. Stick to cabbage soup diet.

Midnight. Bed.

Maximum activity. Minimum food. Busy, fit, full of energy and happy.

I am the same person. I just make different decisions. The change in my body allows me to make different decisions.

This is my average day in Jan 2011

(Add full-time work to the mix of two children and living in a nuclear family)

6.30 a.m. Up with the kids. Deal with school tantrums.

7.00 a.m. Tea and papers.

7.15 a.m. Workout with personal trainer.

9.30 a.m. Breakfast of two egg-white omelet and one brown toast in the car.

9.50 a.m. Reach work.

10.00 a.m. First meeting and then back-to-back meetings all day.

11.00 a.m. Skinny cappuccino or office coffee (not pre-mixed Nescafé).

Noon. Plate of cut mixed fruit.

2.00 p.m. Steamed matra kulcha takeaway from Haldiram. On an indulgent day, chaat as well. To end on a sweet note, pop a sugarfree gum ino my mouth.

4.00 p.m. Start trying to leave for home.

5.00 p.m. Manage to get home.

5.30 p.m. Tea or cold coffee with skimmed milk and one or two digestive biscuits or diet soya snacks.

6.30 p.m. Give the children a bath.

7.15 p.m. Eat dinner with the children.

8.00 p.m. Story and sleep time.

9.00 p.m. Fruit, yoghurt and tea. Catch up with email.

Midnight. Bed.

Maximum activity. Minimum food. Busy, fit, full of energy and happy.

Putting on weight and putting off your life

I was putting on weight and putting off my life. 'I will do this when I get thin.' It became an excuse for everything that was too hard or that I did not want to do.

I'll scuba dive when I am thin because who can fit into a wet suit?

I'll go on a sea plane when I am thin because who is going to reveal their weight to the handsome pilot?

I'll go to the reunion when I am thin because who wants to answer all the 'Why are you so fat? What happened to you' questions?

I'll go to the uber-cool party when I am thin because who is going to wear an unfashionable kurti amongst the glitterati?

I'll speak my mind when I am thin because who wants to stand up and direct everybody's attention in the room to themselves?

I'll do everything when I am thin.

My life was on hold. The list of things I put off for when I became thin was endless. I have no excuses now. Because now I am thin. I can't hide behind my weight. I can do the things I always wanted to do and have to do some of the things I don't really want to.

Hips do lie

There is no inch loss without weight loss. It's hogwash. I have not lost any weight on the scale but my clothes are fitting better. I feel more toned. No change on the scale is a fact. 'I feel like I have lost inches' is fiction unless you are taking the tape out.

Muscle is heavier than fat, so even if you have not lost any weight your jeans can still feel loose. True enough but not good enough. Do not be satisfied with clothes feeling more comfortable. The weight must drop.

Mirror, mirror on the wall, I am not fat at all

The mirror lies. I don't know how this works scientifically, but it lies. You cannot trust it. Now, 40 kg lighter, I still look the same to myself in the mirror. Which, of course, is impossible. I am physically half the person I was. And if you were in front of me you would say I was fishing for compliments, but I honestly think I looked hotter in those days.

Mad? Yes. True? Yes.

When I looked in the mirror at 104 kg, I thought I looked good. I liked my face. And I thought to myself, I still have a thin waist (this is at 43 inches, how delusional can a person be!). Of course, I realized things were not great but, hey, they were not that bad. I could not understand what all the fuss over my weight was about.

But I could not look at pictures of myself. I liked myself in the mirror, hated myself in pictures. I can't explain it. Perhaps we look at ourselves with rose-tinted glasses when we look in the mirror. It's a projection rather than a reflection. It must be a survival mechanism. When I was on the fat side of the yo-yo, my brain switched off the objective part that judged my appearance. Now that I am on the other side of the yo-yo it is switched on high mode, and even though I can practically see my bones, it is not good enough.

I don't look in the mirror now to judge how I look. I wait for the pictures; they tell the real story.

> Not feeling motivated enough to start your diet? Get yourself to a photo studio and photograph yourself. And do it every month. My passport-size photos tell their own story. Sad and hilarious. Take a look at the back cover.

Guilty pleasures

Bones. Those hidden things that hold us up. Wow, really, how good do they feel? I often finish for the day at midnight and when I get into bed I run my finger over my torso and my sides. The hardness of the ribs, the sharpness of my hip bones, the fragility of my collar bones, my wrist… they just feel so good. Don't worry, I am not going into a Meg Ryan orgasm routine. But you get the picture. Kate Moss famously said, 'Nothing tastes as good as skinny feels.' I am sure this is what she meant.

But dieticians don't tell you this. They don't know. When you are fat, your entire body is one soft, lumpy bump. Nothing is sharp, chiselled, hard. Bones are truly a guilty pleasure you should indulge in.

Dieting till you die

How long do I have to be on this diet?

All your life. This may not be the answer you want to hear, but it's the truth.

Dieting is not a short-term activity. Being conscious of your weight is a lifestyle change. This doesn't mean you are always on a diet. Never drinking and never eating are boring. Dieting simply means you let go but you pull back in time.

1

THERE IS NO SUCH THING AS BABY FAT

I was always chubby. Everyone said, Baby fat, how cute. Look at the dimpled thighs and the cushy bottom. Coochie coo! It will all go. No, it won't. It didn't. Here are the nuts-and-bolts or chocolate-and-cheese of how the kilos piled on. And how they came off. And back on again.

JAM TOAST DIET

I was on my first diet at the age of four. Before you call social services for child cruelty, let me tell you that I was 3'4" and weighed 32 kg. If my parents had not put me on a diet, you should have called social services. In any case, there is no such thing as social services in India, unless you consider the friendly neighbourhood aunty or nosy relatives. Everyone who is remotely acquainted with you feels he or she has the right to comment on your weight. If they can see it, they think they can talk about it. Weight is a very personal issue. Someone forgot to tell the neighbours that. So they carried forth with great diligence, constantly commenting on what a healthy child I was, with *so cute* baby fat.

Life was good. On winter mornings I woke up to the smell of halwa. On summer afternoons I stripped down to my white socks and buckled shoes so I could suck on chusa mangoes in peace. Not for long. My mother, who was wearing a bikini when she was five months pregnant with me, knew better. And thus was invented the jam-toast-Tobu-tricycle diet. The principle was simple. If I did ten rounds of the driveway on my red plastic Tobu tricycle, I could have one strawberry-jam toast. Every weekend, early in the morning, the plastic tricycle would start squeaking around the driveway under my ample weight. The whole neighbourhood knew the jam toasts were being earned. Simplistic as it may sound, this is the very foundation of losing weight. You have to earn the privilege to eat yummy food.

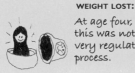

WEIGHT LOST:
At age four, this was not a very regulated process.

WISDOM GAINED:
There is no such thing as a free breakfast.

DIET #2 ● AGE 5 ● WEIGHT 34 KG

DIVINE DIET

The house I grew up in was near a temple on a hill. We woke up in the morning to the sound of bells and were often kept up all night with jaagrans. I was fascinated by the temple and its goings-on. It was a daily ritual to go to the temple with the nanny, heads covered with gaudy red and gold gota chunnis, thalis in hand decorated with flowers. We would get our foreheads plastered with red tikas and ask for double helpings of prasad.

All gods had their special days and their own prasad. Monday was Shivji with white sugar patasa, Tuesday was Hanumanji with orange, sticky, sweet boondi full of ghee, Thursday was Vishnu with melt-in-the-mouth besan laddoos, and Friday was gur channa from Santoshi ma.

This was guilt-free eating since prasad was a divine blessing and did not have calories. True or not, I was an ardent believer. I ate religiously with devout fervor. I was being blessed by the lord himself. And no cycling was required to earn these sweet treats.

WEIGHT LOST:
None

WISDOM GAINED:
Many gods, many treats. Divine food is calorie-less.

DIET #3 ● AGE 7 ● WEIGHT 40 KG

SUMMER FATATION DIET

Other kids had competitions on who could jump the highest or run the fastest. When my cousins and I got together, our competitions were food competitions. Our adda was at my masi's house in Delhi. She has a large kitchen with an eating counter. At lunch time, we would form teams – my cousin sister and I in one and my sister and cousin brother in the other. We would get thalis, load up, on-your-marks-get-set, and shovel till the first one was ready to burst. One time, this game got so out of hand we finished the entire consignment of rajma-chawal made for the house. Counting the staff, this was made for six adults and four children. Another time we ate homemade dosas from lunch time till four p.m., finally stopping only when the batter finished.

One Sunday, as a special treat, we were taken to a newly introduced buffet brunch. This was on the rooftop of a hotel with a super luxurious buffet spread that stretched at least half a mile. We were very excited. Eat as much as you like. We piled up high, wide and deep. And we were instructed by my masi to go back at least three times: starters, mains and dessert. Like we needed encouragement. The under-fives ate for free and the under-tens for half price. We were all under ten, but seeing our stellar performance the staff decided to charge us full price.

We remained undeterred and committed to our cause. And proud of our achievement. When we spent our summers together, we sometimes had these competitions every single day.

The Diet Never to Follow

Wake up: Giant glass of full-fat milk stirred with heaps of Bournvita. Stroll around in the wooded area behind the house. Exercise done.

Breakfast: Toast with thick slabs of homemade white butter. The butter was not spread. The thick slabs were simply laid on top of the toast. Accompanied by a fried egg.

Swim in the pool at the house.

Lunch: Food competition. Mounds of rice, dal, sabzi and dahi.

Snack: Trees of mangoes and bananas.

Teatime: Giant glass of full-fat milk stirred with heaps of Bournvita.

Dinner: Fish fingers or fried chicken with super thin French fries and tons of tomato ketchup. Usually with butter sandwiches and green peas on the side. Apple pie with cream for dessert.

Bedtime snack: Late night drive and ice-cream at GK-1 market or India Gate. Ice-cream was always kasata or bonbons. No low-calorie ice-lollies for me.

Follow this for one month and you are guaranteed to get into the wrong shape.

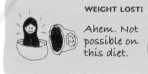

WEIGHT LOST: Ahem. Not possible on this diet.

WISDOM GAINED: Holding a world record in eating rajma-chawal is not conducive to weight loss.

DIET #4 ● AGE 8 ● WEIGHT 42 KG

TIFFIN RAIDER

At age six, I was tricking my best friend into giving me her tiffin. How did that work? Her father was the first general manager of a new five-star hotel in the city, a perk that was completely lost on my slim and beautiful friend. She hated food and her tiffin would be full of candy-coloured petit fours in strawberry pink, vanilla white, lemon yellow and chocolate. This is not my imagination: her tiffin was always a gourmet's delight as it was packed by the hotel chefs! I negotiated so that she could drink from my water bottle and I could eat her tiffin. It was a win-win. She did not want to eat her tiffin but had to show an empty box when she got home while I wanted to devour her tiffin the minute I saw it.

In later years, when other kids got smart and such tactics no longer worked, I took to tiffin raiding. I could not do this daily, only on the days when we had an activity that required everybody to be out of the class. You went to the activity. You sneaked back early into class. You found others' tiffin. Modus operandi: Open. Smell. Taste. Dump or eat.

Some of the tiffin was just delicious. I have never eaten better mini dosas with red chutney and gun powder and little pots of ghee. As though this mother really wanted her little boy to have an authentic south Indian meal. While my own mother was packing me jam sandwiches without butter. By the time I got to my tiffin – which was at my bus stop on my way to school (yes, five minutes after leaving my house!) – the sandwiches were dry and curling at the ends. I still ate them. Better then than later.

The adventures of the tiffin raider did not always turn up gourmet gems. Once, I discovered gajar ke halwa ka sandwiches. Fusion or confusion? Either way, tiffin raiding totally nullified my mother's attempts to control my calories. And I was already hugely overweight.

WEIGHT LOST:
Nada

WISDOM GAINED:
You can take the fat out of the tiffin but you can't take the fatty away from the tiffin.

DIET #5 ● AGE 8 ● WEIGHT 45 KG

SCARSDALE DIET

My parents were fad dieters. They did the Scarsdale diet together. I was also part of this family diet. I can't remember whether I volunteered or was just roped in. This was *the* diet in the eighties. It promised to make you lose 10 kg in two weeks on quite a reasonable amount of food. I just remember the toast and grapefruit in the morning and the brown rice chowmein on Sunday. The rest is a blur. I recently Googled the diet, which claims to be the predecessor of Aitkens and a far healthier version because it includes some complex carbohydrates and fruit. It's basically a high protein/low carbohydrate diet. It was quite revolutionary at the time and when the diet book was published in 1979, it became an immediate bestseller. All I know is that the meal plans and recipes made it fun to do. I don't know whether I lost any weight on it. I was about eight, so I was just doing it because everyone else at home was. But that made it more fun because we were all in it together. It is a fourteen-day plan and has many versions. We followed the vegetarian one.

WEIGHT LOST:
Not sure because nobody weighed themselves.

WISDOM GAINED:
Dieting as a family can be a picnic.

DIET #6 ● AGE 8 ● WEIGHT 45 KG

THE GRAND BREAKFAST

My grandfather was a real foodie. His favourites were not restricted to local produce but came from different parts of the world. Now that doesn't seem like a big deal. But in those days there was one flight a week from Delhi to London and travelling was a huge affair. The entire family would come to say goodbye and my grandmother always gave elaichi-mishri in a small pouch for good luck. Imported foodstuff was not easily available, either. So my grandfather had honeydew melon flown in from London, Sarda melon trucked from Pakistan, bitter marmalade from France, wheatgerm from the US, fudge from the Cotswold, and smoked salmon and shortbread from Scotland. When he travelled abroad he brought back suitcases of fancy cereals and Swiss chocolates.

My grandparents had a chocolate fridge. It was always full of giant bars of Lindt, boxes of mini Roses, tins of Quality Street Sweets and Toblerone. The tradition of the chocolate fridge continues in my parents' house. This long-standing tradition has thankfully been broken in my house. Besides the chocolate fridge, there was also a cookie cupboard. Chocolate cookies with frill edges with big drops of chocolate fondant filled with apricot jam. This tradition has also been broken in my house.

Food was serious business at my grandparents'. Whole Sundays were spent cooking and eating. My grandfather and his food buddies would wake up and go shooting and bring back bater (partridge). Aided by several cans of cold beer, they would spend most of the afternoon cooking a delicious curry. Other friends joined late in the evening with authentic biryani from Old Delhi. And everyone ate together.

I loved spending weekends with my grandfather. Breakfast was our ritual time together. Everything had to be done slowly and with ceremony. We treated each dish like a course. It began with a small bowl of peeled almonds. Then I took my time choosing from the Kellogg's variety pack, even though I knew my choice before I sat at the table. Frosties. It was teamed with hot milk and sliced banana. This was followed by fried eggs with brown toast. The bread was softly toasted and lathered in butter. After this, a glass of freshly squeezed orange juice. And then a glass of milk just for me, in case I had missed out on any essential nutrients.

WEIGHT LOST:
None

WISDOM GAINED:
Maybe love for food is genetic. Nature or nurture?

DIET #7 ● AGE 11 ● WEIGHT 57 KG

BAKING MY CAKE AND EATING IT TOO

In my tweens, I discovered baking. It was the best play activity ever. You baked all afternoon and spent the evening eating your cake and basking in the glory of your superb talent. It is a skill. Don't dismiss it.

My first attempt at baking a cake was layering white bread with Hershey's chocolate sauce and putting it in the fridge, hoping it would become cake. From there to baking cakes in the oven was quite a journey. Rainbow cakes are the most fun to make. The recipe is simple. I still remember it, though this might be due to overuse rather than simplicity!

I had cake tins in all shapes and sizes. Stars, hearts, aeroplanes. The cake looked plain on the outside and when you cut it open, it had all the colours of a rainbow. The freshly baked smell got everyone excited and we all ate cake. The biggest share always went to the baker.

RAINBOW CAKE

1 cup **oil**
1 cup **flour**
1 cup **sugar**
4 **eggs**
½ tsp **baking powder**
Food colour essences in different colours

DIRECTIONS
Beat the eggs, mix in the sugar, then the oil, and finally the flour. Once the batter is ready, pour in equal amounts into several bowls. Add a few drops of essence, a different colour for each bowl. Pour the batter into the cake tin, by adding a spoon from each bowl until you have used all the batter. Bake for 30 minutes.

I was passionate about my new hobby. Even my penpal profile proudly listed baking as my favourite hobby. Though, if I was being honest, I would have to list eating as my favourite hobby.

Anyway, my baking became quite sophisticated over time. My grandfather ate only the finest Scottish shortbread brought all the way from, well, Scotland. There were no Khan Market shops stocked with the choicest foreign biscuits and cookies. As an alternate supply, I found this amazing recipe and started baking (and eating!) shortbread for him. It was really quite professional, with petticoat borders and the finest butter. My grandfather loved it and the whole colony heard about it. After that I baked shortbread for him regularly, always taking a generous cut for it.

WEIGHT LOST:
None

WISDOM GAINED:
Being the star baker of your colony will get you points with the neighbours but not with the weighing scale.

WORKOUT #8 ● AGE 11 ● WEIGHT 56 KG

NOT LAZY, JUST FAT

The thing is, I was overweight but I was never lazy. When I was a child I played pitho (seven-tiles) in the colony. I was obsessed with dogs and was constantly taking them for walks and teaching them to show jump. A theme borrowed from my other love: horse-riding. I would create show-jumping courses in our garden out of anything I could find – chairs, mops, the guard's danda, flowerpots, you name it – and then drag the dogs and myself over the jumps. We would organize dog shows in our garden with rosettes and invites. I was a keen horse-rider and rode daily. It's not the best of exercises, but at least it got me out of the house every day. I also played badminton in the colony. We had a court on the terrace of our house and one in my grandparents' colony park. I was pretty good.

The point of telling you all this is that I was not a slob. The weight must have come on just because I ate too much and probably did not have the best metabolic rate.

DIET #9 ● AGE 12 ● WEIGHT 68 KG

THE VAID FROM PALWAL

When all else fails, turn to traditional wisdom. Enter the Vaid. The aunty from the park knew the aunty from the neighbouring colony who knew of this wonderful Vaid who could cure cancer, so what was a little baby fat. So off we went to the find the Vaid, on the dusty tracks into the deep interiors. The Vaid sat in a small town in a pink house with an attached garage and a cow shed. He was old and shiny, wore a white pagri and was surrounded by people and bottles. He took one look at me and said that I had low blood content. There wasn't enough blood in my system to push the fat out. I did not understand it then and don't understand it now but who knows, maybe things were lost in translation. He made me many packets of different coloured powders – white, brown, black – to be mixed in water, honey, milk and consumed at different times of the day. *Jadoo ki puriyas!*

He told me, 'You urban people are putting on weight because you have stopped doing your own work and stopped squatting to go to the toilet.' According to him, if we continued to squat to make rotis on the chula, do our own poncha and answer nature's call, we would not be fat. The squatting and cooking, squatting and cleaning, I buy, but the argument that our style of chamber pots causes thunder thighs is a little hard to swallow.

He suggested I add poncha as an exercise to the jadoo ki puriyas routine. At least one room in the house had to be swabbed by me every day. Tried and tested, I have to admit this is an excellent exercise. I would sweep the floor to *Wham*! Yes, George Michael. I would put on the music, get a clean poncha and sweep the entire room on my haunches. It also worked out my arms as they had to move the cloth from one side to the other. By the end of the workout, I could barely stand. In ten minutes, I was done and so was the room.

It worked. I lost weight and in all the right places.

But it wasn't just the Vaid's doing. I was highly motivated. I was by now horse-crazy and wanted this fancy saddle, a Stübben. The stunning leather saddle was brought all the way from England and put in my room on a special stand as motivation for losing weight. I would see it first thing in the morning and last thing at night.

WEIGHT LOST:
8 kg

WISDOM GAINED:
Swabbing is great exercise for the hips and thighs. And a little bit of motivation always helps the weight go down.

DIET #10 ● AGE 14 ● WEIGHT 75 KG

FASHION FONDA

I have one word for you: leotards. A leotard, for the uninitiated, is like a skin-tight bodysuit originally designed by an acrobat for easy movement. You wear lycra tights and a swimsuit-type bodysuit on top. And you have matching leg warmers. I had all kind of scary combinations – a pink tiger-stripe costume with black tights and pink leg warmers and pink high-top shoes; black tights, black costume and rainbow leg warmers. I was a vision in lycra.

And there was more to the gear. Headbands. Now let us not overlook the fashion possibilities of the headband. I always wanted Wonder Woman's red band with the yellow star. Of course, the really fit aerobicistas worked out in a leotard bodysuit and leg warmers, with no tights, just toned, bare legs. How much we have all learnt since those days. Workout gear is now non-fussy and not so intimidating. I mean, you had to lose weight before you could get into the gear to do the workout that would make you lose weight.

In any case, aerobics was the rage in the eighties. It was either aerobics or the shake-it-up-baby machine. You put a thick band around the problem area, switched on the machine and it just gave that body part a solid shake. The idea was that the fat would be broken down. In my case, the machine was not an option as I was too young. It was either poncha or Fonda. No prizes for guessing which one I chose.

The Jane Fonda workout video was the golden standard of aerobics. Every aerobicista worth her leotard was doing it. I was twelve and Jane Fonda looked like a goddess. My mom and I used to do it together. We would clear the living area and play the video and follow the workout. It was simple once you had done it about ten times and got the coordination right. It didn't look pretty but it did the job. I gave up on the workout only when the videotape did. With the workout and a healthy diet, I managed to lose quite a few kilos.

The Jane Fonda workout is still one of the most successful home videos ever sold. She re-released it in 2010. Now, when I look back at the video, she looks like an eighties' disco star. Even by today's definition of 'fit', her shape and form are perfect.

WEIGHT LOST:
A fair amount

WISDOM GAINED:
Never ever wear a leotard unless you are Jane Fonda. In fashion or outside it!

DIET #11 ● AGE 16 ● WEIGHT 70 KG

KUAN SESSIONS

In my sweet sixteens, my gang and I invented what we called kuan sessions. These were basically eating sessions where our tummies were akin to bottomless wells. This is a really good metaphor for what transpired in those sessions.

A regular kuan session normally took place at teatime and involved cold coffee with extra sugar and ice-cream. French fries with chilli garlic sauce. Pure Magic chocolate biscuits. Chutney and buttered toast. Chicken salad sandwiches. Leftover lasagna and other random bits from lunch. Crax. Fryums. Chips with cream-cheese spread used as a dip. Dairy Milk chocolate. All in abundance. We would faff and feast, discussing the day we had spent with each other. We affectionately called each other 'thusams'. Stuffers. We were proud of our insatiable appetites.

School canteen food was awesome. Greasy, fatty, delicious. I still remember the crispy brown flaky patties accompanied with sauce in a squeezey bottle. I didn't know then that the extra flavour in that sauce came not from tomatoes but from pumpkin. When I was pregnant that was all I craved – patties with kaddu sauce. Other delicacies of this canteen were white bun burgers smeared with oil or butter with a potato patty and a slice of red onion. With limited pocket money, we had to either rely on others to treat us or share. The canteen was not good for the diet and was outside the control of my first and most fearsome dietician, my mother.

WEIGHT LOST:
None

WISDOM GAINED:
Thinking of your stomach as an endless pit is not a winning strategy.

DIET #12 ● AGE 16 ● WEIGHT 68 KG

CHEMICAL REACTION DIET

This one actually began as a chemical reaction in my brain. A reaction called loooove. Sound cheesy? I know, but that's teenage love for you. I had met a boy. And for boy to look at girl, girl would have to lose some. Sorry, politically incorrect, but hey, I don't make the harsh rules of high school. The kuan sessions ran dry and a new, very effective diet was taken on board.

This diet guaranteed weight loss. Two and a half kilos in three days. You had to follow the diet exactly as it was stated. The mixing of different food groups creates a chemical reaction in the body, which nullifies the caloric intake. You do it for three days and then you get four days off before you start the diet again.

The absurd menus included a tablespoon of peanut butter with grapefruit for breakfast; a cup of boiled beetroot and black coffee for lunch; a cup of tuna, slices of tomato and a cup of ice-cream for dinner.

I hated tuna. I hated peanut butter. I hated black coffee. I would swallow spoons of tuna and peanut butter with big gulps of water. But I loved the ice-cream. It was worth eating strange combinations all day long to be rewarded with a cup of vanilla ice-cream in the evening. I sprinkled mine with coffee powder to create the most delicious dessert.

Chemical Reaction Diet

Salt and pepper are the only recommended seasonings. Drink lots of water – at least 6–8 glasses a day.

DAY ONE
Breakfast: 1 tbsp peanut butter with 1 slice of toast, half a grapefruit, 1 cup black coffee
Lunch: 1 tbsp peanut butter with 1 slice of toast, half cup tuna, 1 cup black coffee
Dinner: 1 skinless chicken breast, 1 cup green beans, 1 cup boiled beetroot, 1 cup vanilla ice-cream, 1 small apple

DAY TWO
Breakfast: 1 boiled or poached egg, 1 slice of toast, half a banana, 1 cup black coffee
Lunch: 1 cup tuna, 6 saltine crackers, 1 cup black coffee
Dinner: 2 Frankfurter hotdogs, half a banana, 1 cup broccoli, half cup boiled carrots, half cup vanilla ice-cream

DAY THREE
Breakfast: 1 slice cheddar cheese, 5 saltine crackers, 1 small apple, 1 cup black coffee
Lunch: 1 boiled or poached egg, 1 slice of toast
Dinner: 1 cup tuna, 1 cup boiled beetroot, 1 cup boiled cauliflower, half cup vanilla ice-cream, half a cantaloupe

But I was all of sixteen then and my tastes have changed since. This diet actually sounds quite appetizing now. If you read the diet carefully, you will see that it has a lot of food in it. Individually, they are all tasty but some of the combinations are totally off.

WEIGHT LOST:
2 kg in 3 days. In total, 6 kg.

WISDOM GAINED:
Fad diets are great if you want to fit into a dress for D day but they don't help if you want to lose 5 kg or more.

DIET #13 ● AGE 16 ● WEIGHT 63 KG

CABBAGE SOUP DIET

This is a seven-day diet and was apparently created in Mayo clinic for heart patients to lose weight quickly. The website now claims it has nothing to do with any hospital or clinic.

This is not a long-term diet. It's more a way to kickstart your weightloss programme. In my best attempt, I did it for two weeks in a row. Fourteen whole days. I don't even want to imagine how I smelt.

The diet involves eating a different food group every day. The only constant is the cabbage soup. This is the killer weapon of the diet. You drink as much cabbage soup as possible. The more you drink, the more you lose. You can have it hot or lukewarm, and for variation I even tried it cold.

The soup can be spicy or lemony, depending on your taste, but after the third day it just starts smelling like garbage and the stench is nauseating. I nicknamed it the garbage soup diet.

The soup was like the Vodafone pug – it followed me wherever I went. In a thermos. In a hip flask. In coffee mugs. I drank it at parties and people around me asked, 'What's that smell?'

Cabbage Soup Diet

DAY ONE

Fruit: Eat all the fruit you want, except bananas. Eat only your soup and the fruit. You can drink unsweetened tea, cranberry juice and water.
It's like a fast day.

DAY TWO

Vegetables: Along with your soup, eat until you are stuffed all fresh, raw or cooked vegetables of your choice. Try to eat green leafy vegetables and stay away from dry beans, peas and corn. For being good, you get a big baked potato with butter for dinner. No fruit today.
With Indian food many tasty vegetarian dishes are possible and you get to end the day with a buttery baked potato.

DAY THREE

Mix days one and two: Eat all the soup, fruit and vegetables you want. No baked potato.
It's still a diet but there is so much variety on this day that it is not too hard.

DAY FOUR

Bananas and skimmed milk: A maximum of eight bananas is allowed. You can drink as many glasses of skimmed milk as you like, along with your soup.
It's a bit of a liquid day but banana milkshakes are a real treat after the soup.

DAY FIVE

Beef and tomatoes: 10–20 ounces beef and up to 6 fresh tomatoes. You need to drink at least 6–8 glasses of water to wash the uric acid from your body. Eat your soup at least once.
I don't eat beef so I substituted with skinless chicken.

DAY SIX

Beef and vegetables: Eat beef and vegetables to your heart's content. You can even have 2 or 3 steaks if you like, with green leafy vegetables. Again, you have to eat your soup at least once.
I replaced this with fish. The soup was making me sick by this point but I gulped it down.

DAY SEVEN

Brown rice, unsweetened fruit juices and vegetables: Again, the diet advises you to stuff yourself. Be sure to eat your soup at least once.
I made myself a nice vegetable pulao as a combination of all permitted foods. And I did not need the diet to tell me to stuff myself.

CABBAGE SOUP

6 large **spring onions** (sliced)
2 **green peppers** (chopped)
1 or 2 cans **tomatoes** (diced or whole)
3 **carrots** (chopped)
1 container (10 oz. or so) **mushrooms** (chopped)
1 bunch **celery** (chopped)
Half a head of **cabbage** (chopped)
1 package spice-only **soup mix**
1 or 2 cubes **bouillon** (optional)
Season to taste with pepper, parsley, curry, garlic powder, etc. and little to NO salt!

DIRECTIONS
Sauté the spring onions in a pot over medium heat until the onions are clearer in colour (about 4-6 minutes).

Add the green pepper to the pot. Add the cabbage, carrots, mushrooms and celery. Add tomatoes now, too.

If you would like a spicy soup, add a small amount of curry powder or cayenne pepper. For seasoning, you can use a spice soup packet of your choice (no noodles!) or use beef or chicken bouillon cubes. These cubes are optional, and you can add spices you like instead (make sure not to add much salt, if at all).

Add about 12 cups water, cover and lower the heat. Let the soup simmer for a long time – about 2 hours or until vegetables are tender.

For a tastier version, add chilli-garlic sauce, soya sauce and a handful of sprouts and peas.

WEIGHT LOST:
First round:
3 kg
Second
round: 2 kg

WISDOM GAINED:
Great kickstart diet. It shocks the system and gets you on track if you can get past the garbage, sorry, cabbage.

DIET #14 • AGE 17 • WEIGHT 68 KG

INDEPENDENCE DAY IN CAMBRIDGE

After my board exams, I went to the UK to prepare for my A-Levels. I was in a sixth-form college in Cambridge, studying to get into Oxford University. This was the first time my food would not be monitored. My live-in dietician, i.e. my mother, was not part of the package. Independence Day was finally here. I wanted to put a little flag on a cupcake (okay, a dozen!), sing myself a song, clap and then eat the cupcake all by myself.

Little did I know that independence with British hostel food is worse than slavery. Lumpy mash, tasteless Yorkshire pudding, stodgy pasta, overboiled Brussels sprouts, soggy carrots, mushy peas. In other words, food hell. Very quickly, I discovered Marks and Spencer's ready-to-eat food. Fresh bread, mixed salads excluding all green leaves and including pasta dunked in fattening dressings. Really, it should not be called salad at all. Forgotten was the hostel food. I would trudge back to my hostel armed with Marks and Spencer's goodies, and because I had no access to a fridge I just hung the bag outside my window. England is always cold enough.

England doesn't just specialize in wet grey weather but also in chocolate. And the one good thing about hostel food was subsidized chocolate. Cadbury's Chocolate Crème Eggs for a few pence. This does not mean I saved money: I just got more chocolate. So, where I would have eaten one chocolate egg after lunch, I ate two.

As I became more familiar with the beautiful university town, I ventured out and discovered the most amazing student hangouts. I loved Aunty's Tea Shop with its cozy interconnected low-ceilinged tea rooms with floral curtains on the windows. Tall cakes thick with butter-cream icing placed on pedestals. Hot scones dotted unevenly with currants and served with little pots of strawberry jam and clotted cream, finger sandwiches with paperthin slices of cucumber and a generous slathering of butter and crushed black pepper. All served in three-tier trays with lace doilies. It was straight out of an Enid Blyton book.

Then there was the famous Cambridge University Death by Chocolate. I can't think of a better way to die. Layer upon layer of chocolate – a base of chocolate biscuits topped with dark chocolate mousse with milk chocolate chips topped with a solid slab of chocolate topped with a moist chocolate cake topped with chocolate butter-cream icing topped with white chocolate curls and served with chocolate sauce. It's a piece of heaven on earth.

And of course there was the student staple, the fish-n-chip shop. They should be called grease shops. Big fat hot chips. There was never a better cure for a cold or a hangover. In retrospect, there was hardly any potato or fish in this specialty, it was just batterfried in the best-quality transfat, flavoured with salt and vinegar and wrapped in a newspaper cone.

As the final exams of my A-Levels approached, I chanced upon the ultimate Cambridge invention to bust stress: the Mars bar toastie. Believe me, this book is worth it for this recipe alone. Delicious and deadly. Many Mars bar toasties were devoured in the name of better grades.

I went through quite a bit of stress-eating in those days. I needed food if I was to cram two years of A-Level work into one year. I needed all the comfort I could get. So I ate and studied and ate some more and that is how it went. I was successful in both. I got into Oxford University and into the fat club in one clean sweep.

MARS BAR TOASTIE

1 **Mars chocolate bar**
2 slices **white bread** or, if you are feeling health-conscious, brown bread
1 grill toaster

DIRECTIONS
Take the chocolate bar, put it safely between two slices of bread, press hard and stick it in the grill.

Toast until the sandwich is grilled and the chocolate and caramel melt and ooze out.

Eat immediately.

Watch it: hot caramel can burn the mouth.

WEIGHT LOST:
Nada

WEIGHT GAINED:
Alpha

WISDOM GAINED:
Full food freedom is not everybody's cup of cream tea!

DIET #15 ● AGE 18 ● WEIGHT 75 KG

THE ROOM WITHOUT A VIEW (OR A CUPBOARD)

I arrived at Oxford University with great pomp and show, coordinated luggage and a fancy car. I was the first person in my family to go to Oxford University. And I was basically given the broom closet as my room. Princess in a closet. You might think it's a joke but it isn't. It was the cleaner's storage room in the student house. They had crammed a bed and a desk into it. There wasn't even room for a cupboard. The cupboard for cleaning liquid and brooms was outside the room and that was cleaned out to give me storage. My mother wept. I ate.

College food was just lard. Tasty lard. And pudding was the tastiest lard. There was pudding every day and drinks every evening, followed by midnight visits to the college tuck shop. By the end of the first term, things were looking (and feeling) quite tight. At university, I had essays to write every week. An essay night meant at least one packet of biscuits and endless cups of coffee. The biscuits were rich – chocolate-covered Hobnobs, Jam Rings, Foxes custard creams – and the coffee was cheap, made with instant coffee powder and Coffee-mate. Coffee-mate, a milk-concentrate, was famous in the student halls for its inflammable properties. If you dropped the powder from a height on a lit match, it burst into a ball of fire. So, with endless cups of coffee, biscuits and mid-air balls of flame for inspiration, I would have an essay, or something resembling it.

I was reading PPE – Politics, Philosophy and Economics – and had three essays a week. You can do the math with regard to the biscuits.

Thanks to the canteen being closed once a week, I also learnt a bit of cooking. Pasta with bottled pasta sauce. The pasta was of the worst kind, white and stodgy, and it was often thrown at the kitchen ceiling to check whether it was cooked to perfection. Every so often, as you tossed yours to the ceiling to test its *al dente* texture, an older fusilli sample would fall into the pot or on your head. It was not the most hygienic of arrangements. But that's student life.

On a good day, some chopped pepper and lots of processed cheese would be added to the pasta. Not exactly health food. But the culinary experience got better. I found small restaurants at student prices and market shops that sold gourmet items. There was Ben's chocolate-chip cookie, which was an excuse of a cookie built around a thick slab of chocolate. And I discovered Häagen Dazs. I have one word for you: Belgian Chocolate Chocolate. I could get through three quarters of a 500 ml tub on my own. And I would stop only out of shame, not out of having had enough.

And if that was not enough, I was introduced to punting picnics. Punts are an Oxford tradition; they are open flatbottom boats with squared ends, used in shallow water. There are no oars; instead, a long pole is used. Who cares, it was just an excuse to have a picnic on a boat. Mostly, we would barely leave the dock and just drop anchor, crack open a bottle of wine and many packets of crisps, cheese, crackers, chocolate.

Needless to say, this university degree was going just one way.

WEIGHT GAINED: A lot

WISDOM GAINED: The first year in Oxford has nothing to do with education. And this advice has nothing to do with weight loss.

DIET #16 ● AGE 18 ● WEIGHT 80 KG

LONG SHOT SPA

Long Shot Spa in Surrey was my first fat farm. It was my second year in Oxford and my mother had decided to take things into her own hands again. I was having a free run at university and it was time to stop the growing trend of my body.

Long Shot was very posh. It was a beautiful old manor in the country, surrounded by woods, brooks and sweeping meadows. The rooms were charming and it had several fitness studios, gyms and a heated swimming pool. Everyone spoke in hushed voices and walked about in fluffy bathrobes. You exercised all day, starting with water aerobics, abs and thigh burner classes, followed by a massage and lunch. Lunch was served in a glass conservatory. The food was uncooked and without a drop of oil. Tasty, healthy but hardly satisfying because the taste of fat is addictive and cannot be substituted. There were all kinds of salads and fruit and herbal teas. After lunch there were more exercise classes and cocktails in the evening followed by a 'thinspirational' talk. Dinner was in the conservatory with the salad bar but there was a hot main course that was brought to the table.

Two weeks of this and I actually lost weight the clean way, with lots of exercise and good, low-fat food.

WEIGHT LOST:
5 kg in 2 weeks

WISDOM GAINED:
When you weigh 80 kg, 5 kg is a drop in the ocean. I looked hideous but felt like a rock star.

DIET #17 ● AGE 18 ● WEIGHT 75 KG

DEAN OF DIETS

The thing about a fat farm is that it removes you from the strains and stresses of real life. In isolation, it is easy to focus on eating right and working out all day. The trick is to be able to do it outside the fat farm bubble.

When I left the Long Shot fat farm, the dietician worked out a diet that I could follow at university, keeping in mind my schedule and the limited food options available to me as a student. I was inspired. I followed the diet for a year and even joined an aerobics class. The instructor was brilliant. She was slim as a bean pole and a little weird. She would draw two red spots on her cheek, just like a clown. I never got it. But she held an aerobics class with 150 people and held it well. I joined the class and really got into it. I cycled to class on my secondhand bicycle or walked or occasionally got driven down by my then boyfriend.

I also volunteered to row for my college. I had to cycle to the Cherwell river on cold mornings and row with numb, red fingers. It was more an excuse to chance upon my sweetheart, who was rowing for his college, than any passion for rowing. I was never very good at it but it got me a good keepsake photo from the Regatta and kept me somewhat fit.

I must admit, the boyfriend was the X factor. It had a lot to do – okay, everything to do – with being able to stay on course. Love had replaced chocolate. This was emotional non-eating, the 'I am so happy I am not hungry' mode.

The Oxford University Diet

Morning: Special K cornflakes with 3–4 strawberries and skimmed milk
Lunch: (picked up from a sandwich shop)
Pita stuffed with 2 tbsp hummus, salad and bellpepper / Camembert cheese baguette with apricot jelly or red onion chutney / Caesar salad with chicken and 1 tsp dressing or low-fat dressing
Tea: Low-fat flavoured yoghurt
Dinner: 8–10 pieces of whole-wheat penne pasta with tomato sauce and vegetables, sugarfree jelly or low-fat flavoured yoghurt.

PLUS
A giant helping of romance.

WEIGHT LOST: 6 kg

WISDOM GAINED:
Gaining a love life can do amazing things to your weight.

2

MY THINNEST POINT

Fifty-five kilos. It lasted all of two days. A bygone era. I can see it so clearly now. The pictures from this time are beautiful. What always strikes me is not just how slim I look but the happy energy that radiates from my face. I was in love.

I finished my degree and moved back to India and got my first job. And carried on an LDR (long distance romance) with my university sweetheart, thanks to the British Airways graduate programme, which gave its employees special deals on tickets. London–Delhi return for just thirty pounds.

He would fly out of Heathrow Friday night after work, get into Delhi early on Saturday morning, leave late Sunday night and go straight to work in London on Monday morning. Most of my friends did not even know he didn't live in Delhi. I was besotted with him and wanted to look my best for him. And I did.

DIET #18 ● AGE 21 ● WEIGHT 70 KG

IDLI SAMBAR DIET

Degree in hand, I landed in Bombay to find my future in the real world. It wasn't as romantic as it sounds. I got my first job as a not-so-hot intern in a hotshot ad agency. It was a four-month programme, at the end of which you got an advertising and marketing diploma certified by the agency. I had never lived in Bombay and found it new and exciting. I travelled by the local Best bus till the plague arrived and then we formed a carpool. I lived with my masi on Pali Hill, she of the gaggle of aunts that specialized in summer fatations. Life was full of advertising lessons by day and group projects by night. And you know what late-night student projects are like – food is an essential member of the group.

My masi is an out-and-out romantic. She loved the LDR story. And finally felt guilty about all the fattening up she had done over my summer vacations. She decided to make amends by finding me a dietician and took it upon herself to monitor my diet. She wanted the first reunion of the LDR to be magical. I had time. The perks of the British Airways programme only kicked in six months after his first day at work.

Udipi Diet

Breakfast: Tea and papaya
Lunch: 2 idlis and sambar, no coconut chutney
Snack: Bhelpuri or tomato and cucumber sandwich
Dinner: Palak raita with a souh Indian tarka

There wasn't any formal exercise as part of the plan. I just walked on the days I could, down Carter Road and around Joggers Park. I found this diet simple and easy to follow. Idli and bhelpuri are easy enough to find in Bombay. It gave me very little excuse to break the diet. It was a bit boring and monotonous but I find that shutting your mind from food in general is essential for the success of a diet. The easier it is to get access to diet food and the less you have to think about organizing it, the less chances there are of breaking it. This diet included all the food groups and super foods like spinach and yoghurt and it made my skin glow. I lost weight and wore a fitted buttoned-down dress in a shade of rich chocolate (my craving was showing up in strange places!) at the graduation party of the diploma course. Finally, I was the hot intern in the hotshot ad agency.

WEIGHT LOST:
8 kg in 10 weeks

WISDOM GAINED:
The diet needs to be simple, even monotonous. Love is a super motivator.

WORKOUT #19 ● AGE 22 ● WEIGHT 62 KG

THE HOME-DELIVERED WORKOUT

The course ended and I was sent to work in the Delhi branch of the advertising agency. I was a copywriter. I worked nine to five except when there was a campaign breaking. Back in Delhi, I kept the weight off by following the diet.

Now that I had lost some of the initial weight, I could add exercise. I got into step aerobics. I bought a step for myself and a workout video. The music was good and the coordination required some skill. But once I learnt the steps – and it took me a while – the workout gave me a real high.

A note on home-video workouts: There are many options out there, depending on the kind of workout you want, the music you like and the trainer you want to be staring at for an hour every day. A six-pack hunk, a Russian blonde, a Bollywood star, a bootcamp general… In fact, why choose? You can get a host of videos, that way you don't have to do the same routine or suffer the same trainer daily.

I think workout videos are a great idea. They are a sort of halfway house to a personal trainer – with less financial commitment and more flexibility in the schedule. You don't have to go anywhere. Someone comes to you, even if virtually. You don't have to push yourself to follow the programme. Most people are too gentle with their workout when they themselves are in control of the repetitions and the level of intensity. With a video, someone forces you to do a fixed routine because you have to follow the video. The level of exercise does not depend on your

My favourite exercise videos:

Jillian Michaels, *30 Day Shred*

The Firm, *Total Body Time-Crunch*

Jari Love, *Get Extremely Ripped!*

mood. It is a really good way to start a regular exercise routine. I think it's easier than going to the gym – there are fewer excuses. All you have to do is commit to putting on the video, and your TV room turns into a gym. And if you can't even be trusted to hit play then, baby, you have a bigger problem.

My Mix-n-Match Diet

Along with the step aerobic workout, I needed to follow a diet. The idli sambar diet was a bit hard to transport to Delhi, so I had to improvise. This diet is owned and controlled by me. I had finally reached a stage where I had the knowhow to create a signature diet of my own. It worked.

Morning: Cold coffee without sugar

Mid-morning: Small bowl of fruit

Lunch: One roti and a bowl of vegetables and yoghurt
Now, I am not a roti person and roti without butter tastes inedible to me. So I got my cook to make the roti as thin and crispy as papad. The vegetables were either bhindi or gobi – no aloo. Lots of chilli.

Tea: Masala chai, 2 Marie biscuits
This tided me over the sweet craving and the low point. There are all kinds of healthy biscuits available in the market; the ragi and oat ones are quite good.

Dinner: Cold coffee with a pear or apple
Weird combo but I loved it.

I did the workout daily. I didn't miss a single day. I am not a morning person so I usually exercised after I came home from work. This was not easy because by evening my body was beat. I had worked all day. I wanted to reward myself with some tasty treats and just chill.

My only tip for curing the too-tired-to-exercise-today syndrome: start planning the mechanics of the workout before you get home. And when you get home, don't sit down to have a cup of tea, catch your breath and tell whoever is listening about your day. Get into your exercise gear. Don't go from work zone to domestic zone. Go straight from work zone to workout zone. Once you are done with the workout then, and only then, call your day to a close. Now you are free to do all the things you want. You have worked and worked out, your day is complete.

WEIGHT LOST: 5 kg

WISDOM GAINED: A sensible diet along with an exercise that you enjoy is the only long-term solution.

DIET #20 ● AGE 23 ● WEIGHT 58 KG
TIPPING POINT

For the final few kilos I joined Personal Point, a pioneer in weight-loss factories. You go in fat, you come out thin. It was a factory of dieticians sitting in little cubicles handing out meal plans and packets of Personal Point snacks. They also had sophisticated vibration machines that made you lose inches. This was India's first attempt at a weightloss centre with before-and-after ads.

I went to the centre twice a week to meet my dietician and to get my treatment. The diet was a simple controlled diet, very much like my own mix-and-match diet, except I replaced my atta for theirs and ate their snacks at teatime. The snacks came in little white packets labelled Personal Point Snack 1, 2, 3… They did not tell you what was inside nor did they give a calorie breakup. The snacks were quite yummy. Rumour had it that they mixed weightloss powders in their atta but I can't be sure. Thankfully, I never had any side-effects like tummy pain or diarrhea.

The treatments were a little shady, though. You were taken into a dark room where you had to strip. A dirty wet towel was slapped over the fatty area (tummy, thighs, hips). A host of straps and pads with little wires and nodes passing electrical currents was tied around you for thirty minutes, twice a week. This made you lose inches by losing fat, or so they said.

The three-pronged approach of controlled diet, tasty low-calorie snacks and inch-loss machines worked. But mostly, I stuck to the programme because I had a deadline, a loveline. I was flying off to South Africa to meet the love of my life, my Oxford sweetheart. We had not seen each other in six months. I wanted him to see me and fall on his knees, on one knee, to be precise. The date was fixed. I had not told him anything about my weightloss programme. With no internet and no mobile phones, it was easy to keep large parts of my life secret. I wanted to surprise him, and I did. And boy, oh boy, did he return the favour.

I looked amazing. Midriff-baring outfits. Tight clothes. Jeans. Bones. Oh, the bones! On the plane to South Africa, I got the jitters. Maybe I didn't look as great as I thought. But then the steward hit on me and upgraded me to business class and I was all set.

We met at the airport in Johannesburg. We might have done the slow-motion Hindi movie run but he ran past me. He didn't realize it was me and the *DDLJ* music did not play on cue, even though his name is Raj and he is from London. It was a rocking start but the reunion was a success, once he recognized me. One evening in Cape Town, I was whisked away on a sunset cruise. It was just the two of us, in a beautiful old boat with a salt-worn wooden deck and spotless white sails. We sat on the deck, wrapped in soft duvets, and sipped champagne as we watched the bright orange sun set against the dark, square, flat-topped Table mountain. Sipping, sailing, sinking into the moment. And then *clank!* Something hard hit my teeth. It was a ring, a South African commitment band. It had a solitary diamond and a black elephant hair inset into the band. Elephant hair in Africa symbolizes longevity and is supposed to possess powers of protection. Unique. Magical. Beautiful. This could be the perfect fairytale ending ... if only the princess could keep her mouth shut.

WEIGHT LOST:
The stubborn last 3 kg

WISDOM GAINED:
Love makes the world go round, so what's a little weight?

DIET #21 ● AGE 24 ● WEIGHT 68 KG

THE WEDDING DIET

I don't know of any girl who has not gone on a wedding diet. Thin or fat. A wedding diet is an essential part of the big day.

When I got engaged, I was at my thinnest. And I had the most romantic marriage proposal. Maybe this is a coincidence. But I think there is a lesson here. You are the most desirable when you are at your thinnest. Well, at least I am. This is not just about looking good, I think it is about feeling good from the inside. You look radiant and you radiate good energy because you are happy. This makes the people around you want to spend time with you for the rest of their lives!

It's a sort of self-fulfilling prophesy. You look like a rock star, you feel like a rock star, you look more like a rock star. But there are some people out there (please do raise your hands) who are not defined by their weight and they can be happy and cheerful even when they are having a fat day or a fat life. Well, I am not one of them. I am defined by my weight.

OLD MAC HITLER HAD A FARM
(…and on that farm he had some fat chicks)

After the yearlong engagement, D day was upon me and in my joy I had piled on the kilos. I had let go. Now I was desperate and time was short. So I decided to give the famous health farm in Bangalore a shot. When I was growing up, I had heard a lot about it. My grandfather was a big fan and my grandmother had been sent – yes, sent – there a couple of times.

It was very much the health capital of the eighties. It was one of a kind, before the plethora of ayurvedic centres, farms and spas came up in south India. The fat and the fashionable were all headed south to lose weight. Anyway, back to my grandmother. She was sent. And all kind of things were sent from Delhi to make life bearable for her at the farm. A whole household was shifted, different family members took turns to be my grandmother's companion at the farm. It was almost like an adult boarding school where you were sent as punishment for putting on too much weight.

In spite of the stories I grew up with, I made the decision to go to the farm a few months before my wedding. I was suffering from bridal stress. I went without a companion and without an entourage of trappings. I thought some alone-time would be good for reflection before I took the plunge.

It wasn't that simple. The farm had a long waiting list. Many strings had to be pulled. Old relationships had to be dug up. The frequent sufferer card (many family members had been many times) had to be brought out before they gave me a place. Somebody out there was looking out for me but I fought against their good will and made it to Old Mac Hitler's Farm.

Have you packed your bags yourself?

At the gates of this sanctuary, they asked some tough security questions. They had perfected the American security procedure pre-Al Qaeda. No food items and medicines allowed. Have you packed these bags yourself? Has anyone tampered with the bags in your absence? Have you been given any gifts to carry? And after I answered all the questions truthfully they frisked me and my bag anyway. It was somewhat intimidating. Not your trademark Thai spa-style *swadika* welcome!

The minute I entered, they weighed me on a quintal machine. This is a weighing machine used for farm animals. No namby-pamby little digital machine for this farm. The farm itself was quite pretty. It bordered a lake, had a nice walking track and luxurious rooms. The room I stayed in was a cottage with en suite facilities and a small sitting room that had a TV. Comfortable enough.

The reich

The morning began with a Nazi-like siren that went off at five a.m. It was still dark outside and loud kirtan (the most unmelodious I have ever heard) blasted from speakers that were hidden in trees throughout the property, especially around the walking track. You had to start the day with one round of the track before breakfast. Umm… breakfast? A glass of coconut water.

Yes, that was the diet. I consumed four glasses of coconut water and took daily enema for three weeks. That was it. Simple and easy. The water was sweet and the coconut was grown on the farm, as were most other vegetables, though I can't really vouch for the rest as I only had coconut water for three weeks.

The dining room was split in two. One for those allowed the low-calorie vegetarian food and a smaller room for the coconut-water drinkers. We were segregated, like smokers and non-smokers. And there was no cheating. You could not slip into the eating zone and get a thali. They were really strict about checking tags. One day, tired of my coconut-water diet, I wanted to have some saunf. Raw, calorie-less, digestive fennel seeds. They said NO. Special permission had to be requested and given by the high command before I was given a spoon of saunf. I repeat, a spoon of saunf.

Did I pass out? No. Did I feel low in energy? No. I was walking three times a day. There was nothing else to do, really. About 6 km a day. Did I feel cranky? Maybe for the first few days and then I just went numb. We, the prisoners, used to keep ourselves going by watching cookery shows on TV. That was our only access to food.

Once, they were showing this amazing recipe for chicken in a mustard cream sauce. That day, I just wanted to jump into the TV and eat up the mustard cream chicken.

CHICKEN IN MUSTARD CREAM SAUCE

2 **chicken fillets**
4 tbsp **butter**
A large fistful of grated **cheese** (cheddar is preferable)
3 tbsp **French wholegrain mustard**
I small tetrapack **cream**
2 **spring onions**, chopped

DIRECTIONS
Boil the chicken fillets in water with a teaspoon of butter. This makes the chicken really soft and gives it a melt-in-the-mouth texture.

Prepare the sauce just before you are ready to eat as it only takes a few minutes.

Heat the remaining butter in a pan, add the chopped spring onions and grated cheese.

Once the onions are a little soft and the cheese is melting, add the mustard.

Finally, add the cream.

Vary the quantity of cheese, cream and mustard, depending on whether you like your sauce creamy, cheesy or sharp.

Watching cookery shows and being on a starvation diet is not the wisest combination. By the way, I did try the recipe many months later, and it turned out delicious. It's really easy to make and even easier to polish off.

The daily torture included heavy massages with the world's smelliest oil (sesame seed oil with Ayurvedic herbs), to remove the cellulite. There was also water therapy, where they stripped you stark naked and stood you against a wall in a dark, empty, windowless room, rather like a gas chamber. Then two scary overweight matronly women wardens would enter and laugh loudly with their white teeth flashing in their dark faces as they aimed high-pressure jets of water on your trouble spots with industrial hoses and sadistic delight.

There were other resemblances to Nazi techniques. They had surprise midnight raids where a loud siren would sound and the authorities would land up to check your rooms for unauthorized food and medicine. They went through all your belongings and turned your suitcases upside down and patted down the lining. It was a genuine search operation, not for the faint-hearted. They found a couple of Crocin in the bag of one of the guests when I was there. She was expelled at once.

Survival

While you were at the farm, you could not leave or enter the premises at will. Once you were checked in, you were committed to the stipulated time. If you broke the bond, you were expelled, never to return.

I survived the farm. We discussed our favourite restaurants and favourite dishes and favourite recipes, but we did not touch food. Dreaming about all the food we could not eat and bitching kept us going. Complaining about the haves (those who could eat at the farm), about the place, about the authorities – that's what kept us sane. This venting was the best kind of therapy.

I think I survived mainly because I had no choice. I could either quit or I could stay and keep my mouth shut. Again, I was highly motivated. I wanted to be a beautiful bride.

The experience was gruelling, to say the least. But there must have been something in the detoxifying technique because three weeks later, I had lost 8 kg and was still standing. Of course, this is not a sustainable diet. You can't live on coconut water. This system is almost impossible to replicate outside the environment of the farm. You need the no-stress, no-stimulation, no-commitment, no-food environment to go on such a restrictive diet for so long. You could possibly do it once a week (and once in your life) as a cleanser. In the josh of my return or on account of severe malnourishment causing temporary madness, I tried to stay on a diet of just juice but that lasted all of two days. Then I returned to a more sensible diet.

The intervention

I call this kind of extreme dieting an intervention. An extreme measure to bring a fat situation under control very quickly. That's what it was. But I learnt something invaluable. My body survived for three weeks. I survived, I was not emaciated. My hair did not fall off. I could still laugh, talk, walk. So if four glasses of coconut water are all it takes for the body to function, we are massively overeating in our regular lives. That's what I realized. You don't need that much food for survival.

The farm made me get over my fear of strict dieting. It broke my conditioning that severe dieting would make me weak, dizzy or low in energy, that I would lose essential nutrients and that it wasn't good for me. Sadly, this is not true. I am not recommending that you try this at home and stop eating. And, of course, extended periods of just coconut water will lead to all of the above, but as a short sharp intervention, I see no harm. Especially if you are very overweight and need a kickstart. What is worse than a severe diet is the overeating that has become part of our daily routine.

Another important thing I learnt is that we do not eat just to create energy for physical activity. I was physically very active – more than in my normal life – at the Nazi farm but survived the non-calorie diet. What I did not have was any mental or emotional strain. In our busy daily lives, I believe we consume calories not just for physical activity but for the mental and emotional activity and stress we take on.

The Nariyal Pani Diet

Breakfast: 1 glass coconut water
Lunch: 1 glass coconut water
Tea: 1 glass coconut water
Dinner: 1 glass coconut water
Extras: daily enema

WEIGHT LOST:
8 kg

WISDOM GAINED:
We need very little food to survive.

3

MAKING UP FOR LOST WEIGHT

After the wedding, I gained gained gained, lost a
little, and gained gained gained. It is my darkest
health period. How did I get from my thinnest
point to my fattest point? Well, I took my time,
about twelve years. There were many changes. I
moved three countries. Changed six jobs.
Shifted five houses. Got one more diploma.
The only constant was food.

AROUND THE WORLD IN EIGHTY KILOS

One-way street, London

I was a beautiful bride. All brides are beautiful but I looked my absolute best. Being thin and being in love – there isn't a combination more deadly or more attractive. After the wedding I moved to London. Our flat was on Oxford Street. I had my investment banker husband's generous credit card and no job. All day, all I did was either plan the dinner I would cook (read: heat in the microwave) or scour restaurant reviews for where we could dine out that night. The rest of the time I shopped. And I had a lot of time. I had no real friends in London. I would make twenty 'when-are-you-coming-home' calls a day to my husband.

I ate to kill time and loneliness. I had got into a state of inertia and lost the motivation to stay healthy. I needed an external force to move me. My husband did try. He said, 'Happy birthday, darling. Here is a gym membership to the uber-luxury gym round the corner.' As it was my first married birthday present, I found this highly inappropriate and it turned into a huge fight. The argument went something like this: 'You think I am fat. This is my first birthday since we got married and this is what you get me?'

In retrospect, this is funny. Like, of course at 5'3" and 80 kg you are fat. My husband should have said, 'Yes, you are and maybe you are blind too.' Of course, if he had said that he would have been killed. Slaughtered. I stress this point because when you are that way, you just don't see it. You don't want anyone else to see it and you definitely don't want anyone to point it out. You think, if you don't see it and accept it, no one else does. But you know what? They all do, they just stop telling you.

My husband said meekly, 'It's a really good gym, baby. Very plush and right next to the house. I thought you might like to have something to do with your day. You don't have to go if you don't want to.'

Now I can look back and say, I was fat and he wanted to put me back on track before I totally lost the plot. He was giving me the right message and I ate up the messenger.

It was non-refundable – no, not the messenger, the gym membership – so I went. I am not sure what I did there. But losing weight was definitely not one of the things.

Hong Kong: Party like it's 1999

A couple of months later, my husband got transferred to Hong Kong. It was the year of the handover to China and there was an economic crisis in Asia. Japan had collapsed. It was a good thing because our personal economy of two had crashed too. We were overspending by a large margin. If they had not sent us to Hong Kong, we would have had to run away to China in any case.

We flew off to Hong Kong to lead the expat life on an expat package. For the uninitiated, the British expats are a rarefied lot who are spoilt by their employers with plush accommodation and a hefty allowance over and above their domestic package, for staying in exotic locales away from the cold grey climes and cramped homes of their own country. We got ourselves a lovely four-bedroom flat with full seaview in midlevels, in a very central and prime area of Hong Kong, from where you basically took an escalator to work. The world's longest escalator. I got a job working for a group that produced a series of free city publications for English tourists and expats. It was a great job as it meant eating at new restaurants, going to Gucci fashion shows and operas in the

Forbidden City and travelling to Macau on a regular basis. It also meant travelling to Guangzhou and reviewing restaurants that looked like zoos. You chose the tastiest animal and waited for it to show up on your plate. So there was the good and the bad.

My diet and exercise plan involved eating too much and working out too little. Breakfast was tea in bed brought by husband dearest (we were still in the honeymoon phase). My work lunches consisted of giant footlongs and sweet treats from a chain of sandwich shops. We had a part-time cook who made our dinner and froze it. And we ate out a lot.

I was expecting to eat Chinese food every day. But Chinese food in China was the real deal and tasted nothing like the Chinese food I was used to in India. They don't bring the rice till the end and the chicken turns up whole with the baby chick's eyes still in place. And chicken feet come with claws. It put me off Chinese food for life. Every Sunday we had a brunch routine which started at noon and went on till four. It was one long feast of breakfast, lunch and tea. The buffet was outstanding and never-ending and I did it full justice.

I joined the famous California gym chain. They had a live DJ at peak hours, multiple studios, hot instructors and row after row of machines. They really did try to make working out fun. But they didn't fool me. Their gyms were famous for innovative group classes such as the body pump where they mix aerobic routines with free weights and ABT (abs, butt and thigh) workouts. I tried everything once, to know I should be doing it, but I was not doing it.

Clothes were becoming a problem. The Chinese are small and the largest size they had was a 12. I couldn't find anything that fit my rotund shape and had to rely on the few options available at Marks and Spencer. That's a real bummer about being oversize, not being able to buy clothes at a store. Shopping always got me down. I couldn't fit into anything and having to stare at myself under glaring light in a full-length mirror in the changing room was hard on the ego. It required a triple scoop at Häagen-Dazs to recover my spirit.

We travelled back to London a few times that year to attend family weddings on my husband's side. I had put on a lot of weight by now. Only nine months had gone by and I could not fit into any of my wedding finery. Freshly tailored lehengas had to be couriered to me from India. They were beautiful but they were extra-extra-large. The wedding was torture. I kept having to deny we were pregnant. That's the done thing in the social structure of the Pendos – first-generation Indians in the UK – you have honeymoon babies. But I was from Delhi, a big city girl, not some village belle from the Pind. Nine months after the wedding, I had the bump but no baby. I was just fat. The Pendos were just as confused as me with this turn of events.

My body survived the family weddings but my ego did not. I went back to Hong Kong and renewed eating with full vigour.

My husband should have put his foot down or sealed my jaw. I know so many husbands like that, they notice every inch their wives put on and give them a hard time about it. I don't think I would have put up with him telling me off about my weight but his unconditional acceptance of me did not work either. I remained happy but deep down I was broken. I had gone from beautiful glowing bride to 'Are you pregnant?' in just nine months. My weight bothered me greatly. I could not, did not, face it. I started to believe it was something I could not change as the problem had become so huge. It made me feel helpless. I took that worry and buried it under mounds of food. I justified it by telling myself that as long as the love of my life loved me the way I was, I could not care less about the world. Bad arse–fat arse attitude. And so the food party in Hong Kong continued.

Viva Vancouver

The expat life and its luxuries soon came to an end. We were transferred back to London after a year. The party was over. It was time to get real. Or to get virtual. The online space was getting hot and I had started dabbling in websites. I decided to take this up more seriously and do a diploma in internet publishing. I chose a course in Vancouver.

The campus at the University of British Columbia was stunning. I could see the sea, mountains, tall trees and snow-capped peaks from my dorm room. The course was tough and the campus lonely. During the week I ate huge chocolate-chip cookies (they were freshly baked on campus, one whiff and you were hooked) and giant mugs of cappuccino for breakfast, followed by sandwiches and Nanaimo bars for lunch. A Nanaimo bar is a Canadian invention. It is nirvana. And you can buy it at the shop next door. It's got a chocolate, nut and cookie base topped with creamy custard topped with a fat slab of dark chocolate. You can get many variations of the custard, the biscuit base and the chocolate on top. All are yummy. Dinner was usually macaroni-and-cheese out of a box, drenched in Tabasco sauce. Talk about lard, carbs and artery blockage. Five kilos for free, just add hot water!

I also discovered other American staples – Miracle Whip, Cheese Whiz and the corn starch syrup that hides in everything edible. These are the evils of our food chain. The worst type of calories you can find.

Needless to say, my food habits were spiralling out of control.

Pudding Lane, London

The course was good and I was in high demand on my return to the UK after four months. I got a job as a web channel developer with a big publishing group that specialized in tech publishing. We moved to a new house by the Thames. I took the ferry to my dockside office. It was perfect. On a perfect English summer's day, smoothie in hand, riding the ferry to work down the Thames, Prada glasses on, hot sun, cool air, I felt blessed. My office was two minutes from the famous gourmet sandwich chain Pret A Manger and I was a happy bunny.

After a lovely lunch by the river, I would stroll over to the supermarket and shop for dinner. In the evening I took the ferry home and then walked along the promenade to our little river cottage and cooked dinner, sipping a glass of wine, listening to Jazz FM in my purple kitchen, watching the occasional boat with fairy lights sail past my kitchen window on which sat my very own herb garden. When my husband came home we sat in our pocket-size bamboo garden, eating dinner by the light of lanterns and the sound of chimes. And then we retired with a tub of ice-cream to the large red couch and snuggled down to watch TV. Everything about my life was picture perfect. Except me.

I was getting uncomfortable in the bucket seat of our little red convertible and the walk down the river was not fun. The chair at work was getting tight and I found the arms digging into my thighs. Overall, these were not good signs. But who was looking?

In London, it was easy to be huge. People were in general bigger. Large size clothes were not hard to find and I had a new set of friends who accepted my new size as me. They did not know any better, they hadn't seen me any thinner. They did not remind me and I conveniently forgot. As long as I could get out of my husband's-side family wedding, I could cruise along at my new weight for a long time.

But I discovered that plane rides had started to give me major palpitations and anxiety. I could not figure it out. I was a seasoned traveller. I had been around the world at the age of eight. I refused to admit it then but it was the width of the seat. I was getting too wide for economy class and being stuck in something too small for eight hours' travel had started giving me major stress. I joined the Weight Watchers programme.

WEIGHT GAINED: 25 kg in 4 years

WISDOM GAINED: Emotional eating can be a silent killer. (But more about that later.)

DIET #23 ● AGE 28 ● WEIGHT 85 KG

WEIGHT WATCHERS

Getting on this programme was my half-hearted effort to try and save the situation. My weight was getting a little out of control and it was starting to alarm my family in Delhi. In London, Weight Watchers is all pervasive. There are support groups, forums, magazines, meetings and it even has its own aisle in the supermarket.

Weight Watchers (WW) is a programme that was started forty years ago by an American woman who discovered that the best way to lose weight was to eat normal food and to be able to share your progress and experience with others. She expanded this simple learning into a worldwide business. They now have a presence across the world. They have about 6000 meetings a week in the UK alone.

Weight Watchers functions on counting points with their proprietary 'point system'. You are given a point budget and have to stay within it. Every food has a point value. The point value is based on the food's calories and saturated fat. You can choose what to eat as long as you stay within your point budget for the week because all calories are not equal. The idea is that 100 calories of a banana, for instance, are not equal to 100 calories of chocolate as the fat content is different, even though the number of calories is the same. Higher fat content in chocolate makes it the wrong, though tastier, choice. The WW point system takes the fat content into account and makes choosing the right food easier. You can choose to use up your points with high-point single items like chocolate but this will leave you with very few points to fill your tummy and day with other foods.

The idea is to make smart food choices, which will last you through the week, rather than bad ones, which will leave you hungry or overdrawn on your point budget.

The diet is based on the premise that denial does not work. On this diet you do not need to deny yourself anything. You can eat dessert. Drink wine. Dine out. You just need to plan. You can plan for special occasions by saving points from another day. There are a few restrictions but you have a week's points to play with.

The freedom in point accounting allows you to live your life and fit the diet around it rather than the other way round. It was not boring or straitjacketed. I had as much variety as I wanted. The programme was flexible and really easy to follow because WW foods are available everywhere in London. There are WW chocolates, snack, bars and microwaveable meals. I never ran out of a WW choice.

Free food!

I love the concept of free food. All fruit and lots of vegetables are free food. With the exception of bananas, mangoes, potatoes, parsnip and sweetcorn, you can eat as much raw fruit and vegetables as you want. They are counted as no calories. Grapes, melons, apples, strawberries, lemon and lime are no calories. Vegetables like broccoli, cucumbers, peppers, pumpkin, beans, spinach and also egg whites are considered free food.

I never bought from the wide list of calorie-free fresh food. Instead, I used the WW excuse to try out all kinds of low-fat goodies. Chocolate bars, biscuits, pancakes, cream. All fat-free but with WW points. This was kind of missing the point. You are not supposed to fill your points with these tasty but not very filling foods. You are supposed to mix it up. Some filling food and some treats. I would eat my point allowance but still stay hungry, which, if you see the sample meal plans, you need never be if you make the right choices.

I could not make the right choices. I was allowed four pieces of ravioli or an entire plate of whole-wheat pasta. I chose ravioli each time. I ate for taste, not to get filled up.

One week was too long a time to let loose a foodaholic like me with calories and points. You need to be highly motivated and self-disciplined. I always thought I would make up today's sins with tomorrow's points but tomorrow never came. By the end of the week, I would have a huge deficit and start making excuses for not going to the weekly WW meeting.

The leaders at the meetings were people who had lost weight with WW and were trained to guide and motivate. But for that, you had to show up! At the meetings they taught you to make smart choices for life. But at that stage in my life, the training was too advanced. I was a baby and far too spoilt. I needed hand holding. I did it seriously for the first two weeks. I attended two meetings and then I gave up. I reassured myself that I had the WW book with all the points and would follow the plan without going to the meetings. Of course I didn't.

Weight busters

But they taught me some great tricks. And these can be used whether or not you are following Weight Watchers.

- Always eat high-volume foods. Apart from fruit, the other satiating high-volume foods include complex carbohydrates that are high in water, air and/or fibre, such as popcorn, vegetables and whole-grains like brown rice.
- Eat more vegetables, such as leafy greens, lettuce, tomatoes, green beans, summer squash and onions. In fact, put them in stews, soups, pasta sauces, pizza and meat loaf. They are high-volume, high-satisfaction, low-calorie superstars because they are loaded with water and fibre.
- Limit very dry foods like pretzels, crackers and chips. Dry foods lack water and thus are low in volume. Dry foods pack a lot of calories into a small portion and are easy to overeat.
- Replace whole milk with fat-free milk.
- Replace juice with fruit.
- Replace aerated drinks with diet aerated drinks.
- Replace potato with yam or sweet potato.
- Eat fruit with the peel to increase the fibre content.

Superstar trick

Replace white with brown. White rice with brown rice. White sugar with brown sugar. White flour pasta with whole-wheat pasta. White salt with brown spices like pepper, cumin, chat masala. White sauce with a red or brown sauce. White bread with whole-wheat bread or chappati.

My first personal trainer

To support my weightloss effort at WW, my husband suggested I get a personal trainer. There was a gym close to our house, but the problem was in getting there. Not logistics, just motivation. The personal trainer's first job was to get me there. This was the first time that I was working out with a trainer. She met me for an hour at the gym three days a week and cost an arm and a leg. She made me do a combination of cardio and calisthenics. She was very sweet but I lost no weight.

The trainer was more committed to her own programme than mine. She was running the London marathon that summer and I was just another job. For me, it was a token attempt at doing something about my weight. I had no idea how to get the most out of a personal trainer.

She could have changed the weight lock but she was not committed to me and I was not committed to her. There were no fixed targets for weight loss. She did not work me hard enough and three days a week is really not enough. So be warned: getting a personal trainer does not equal weight loss. You need to be motivated, and the trainer needs to be trained.

WEIGHT LOST (VERY LITTLE):

2 kg

WISDOM GAINED (A LOT):

A weightloss programme is only as good as your motivation to follow it.

HOW DO YOU GET FAT?

How I got from 60 to 88 kg is a bit of a blur. That it is a blur is a sign in itself. I was totally mindless about my body and health at the time. Now I can spot others who are in that same zone. Once you are there, you just don't think about your weight.

Telltale Signs that You Are in the Fat Zone

- You shy away from being photographed
- You don't like going out
- You are living in a few clothes even though your cupboard is full
- You need to take off your clothes the minute you get home as you are most comfortable in your pyjamas
- You plan your life around what you are going to eat rather than the people you are going to meet
- You stay clear of any topic involving weight, diet, exercise
- You don't like to meet people you have not met in a long time
- You never climb onto a weighing scale
- You are uncomfortable in an economy seat

People say losing weight is one of the hardest things to do, and it is. But putting on weight is not that easy either. It's actually much harder. If I look at my track record, it took me far longer to put on weight than to lose it. It took me eleven years of uncontrolled eating to put it on and about eighteen months of focus to lose it and stabilize it. Of course, putting it on is far more enjoyable. You are in bliss, picking and putting in your mouth whatever you please.

Here are the signposts to getting fat:

Mindless eating

Systematically and relentlessly following a full-on eating and no-exercise plan, I ate dessert twice a day. I devoured chocolate at will. At restaurants, I smothered the bread from the bread basket with butter. I ate French fries with barbeque sauce as a snack. I tried every dish at the buffet. I added cubes of sugar to my cappuccino.

I was on a six-meals-or-more plan. I ate every meal and all the snacks in between. I never thought about what went into my body. Butter, chocolate, bread. Whatever the heart desired went straight in. I never thought about compensating. And never moved a limb.

Happily married

Happiness has a shape and it's not thin. I wouldn't dismiss the old wives' tale that happiness gives you a healthy glow. I was deliriously happy. I had married my childhood sweetheart. We were living in a cutesy picture-perfect house of our own. It was a fairytale life. Unfortunately, I have no photos to prove this as I would not let anyone with a camera near me. The reality of a photograph is like the stroke of midnight when the princess becomes a pumpkin.

When you are happily married and content, something in you loosens, and you don't care as much. Maybe it's a natural human tendency. Your body is designed to find a mate and when it does, and the matter is sealed, it slackens. I have seen many married women put on weight. Even the skinny ones.

Homesickness

I attribute the massive weight gain to the change in my home environment. My regular diet and climate had changed completely. From sunny India to grey UK. It was too cold to do anything but eat comfort food. I was eating bread, pasta and potatoes, which I ate very little of in my Delhi life. And also chocolate. Lots of chocolate and biscuits. London is full of chocolate. You go to the train station, the supermarket, the office ... you just can't get away from it.

Also, there was suddenly a lot of processed food in my diet. I was great at opening jars of pre-cooked food and sticking things into the microwave. This was the era of TV-tray dinners and there were many exciting options. I didn't read the fine print. They were full of calories and fat to make them taste good.

It did not help that I did not know how to cook. I could not even make masala chai. Toast and teabag tea was all I could make when I got married. Slowly, I learnt. My best cooking trick: when in doubt, add cream, butter and olive oil. This works well on the tastebuds but not on the butt.

In the West, even fresh food, unless it is organic, contains many preservatives, which does not help with weight control. The fact that a fruit can look perfect and juicy even after several weeks is an indicator of the amount of preservatives it probably contains.

And wine. Suddenly, after regulated Delhi, I had access to good wine and we cracked open a bottle every day.

More than anything, I think I was just homesick and did not know it. Away from friends and family, cut off from my emotional support system, transported into an alien environment, doing alien things – washing, ironing, cooking, vacuuming. I was lonely and somewhere deep down I was filling that gap with food. I wasn't unhappy, maybe just unrooted or uprooted. And this must be true in varying degrees for most women who get married and move homes and adapt to a new life.

I can be fat, nobody knows me here

Being away from friends and family can be very liberating. It's similar to being able to dress differently when you are away from home. There is no one to tell you the way it is. Plugging into a new network allows you to be whoever you want to be or, in my case, whichever weight I wanted to be. There was no one to tell me I was fat, no reminders of the slim me, and no motivation to go back to it.

XL please

As long as you can find clothes you can fit into, you feel you are not fat. In London, fashionable oversized clothes are easy to come by. They have special shops for plus sizes and several high-street brands go up to size 18. This makes shopping less stressful and takes your focus away from your weight. I spent many months in black XL Gap T-shirts and boot-leg stretchpants. I had them in dozens. They are comfortable and black and create the illusion that you are thin.

Rewards

I developed this warped concept of rewards. I believed I needed to reward myself for every effort I made. Naturally, the reward was an edible treat. If I went shopping for groceries, I rewarded myself with a bar of chocolate. If I went to work in the tube, I rewarded myself with a coffee and a muffin or flapjack.

Don't you dare go there

I never climbed onto a weighing scale. My friends tell me they were afraid of the road I was going down. Every time I visited Delhi from London, they were shocked at the weight gain. They were scared for me but too scared to tell me. One friend says he had to ban the word 'tun tun' (fatso) and all such references from his vocabulary. It was stressful being around me because they were out partying, eating and drinking with me when deep down they believed it was the last thing I should be doing. Now they tell me.

I would never talk about my weight in those days. My husband did not know my weight. I did not tell him. Hey, most of the time, even I did not know my weight. I would not go anywhere near the machine that lied! Any attempt by family and friends to find out my weight was crushed. The topic was changed. The conversation would take another course.

Self Fat Test

Take a minute to find out if you are in danger zone

- ☐ Do you usually eat bread and butter at restaurants?
- ☐ Do you always order dessert?
- ☐ Do you order a cappuccino after dessert and add sugar to it?
- ☐ Do you drink and also eat the cocktail snacks?
- ☐ Do you feel too full after a meal and want to sleep straight after?
- ☐ Do you plan your day around the food you are going to eat rather than anything else?
- ☐ Do you drink more than two non-diet aerated drinks a day?
- ☐ Are most of your clothes a few sizes too small?
- ☐ Is your wardrobe mainly black?

If the answer to at least four of the questions above is YES, you are in the fat zone

- ☐ Do you ever think of compensating for indulgences?
- ☐ Do you weigh yourself daily or even once a week?
- ☐ Do you know your own weight?
- ☐ Does anyone else know your weight?

If the answer to any of the questions above is NO, you are in the fat zone

WEIGHT GAINED:

25 kg

STATE OF BEING:

Deliriously happy to start with and not hugely happy to end with.

WISDOM GAINED:

It's really easy to put on weight but if you really think about it, it takes far longer to gain weight than to lose it.

4

DOUBLE INCHES, NO KIDS

I was now frighteningly fat and a family
intervention was planned to airlift me to Delhi.
Unlike London, I was not anonymous in Delhi.
And I was not allowed to rest on my
lovely fifty-six-inch hips.

At first I resisted. But then it happened, one fine evening, on my way back home from the Tesco supermarket. Two heavy bags were held in one hand with numb fingers, another bag cut into my arm, leaving my other hand free to hold the umbrella. I was walking in slush with the cold rain pouring around me, a howling wind biting at my cheeks, and if that was not bad enough, my umbrella turned inside out and the plastic bags gave up and so did my will to live. I had had enough of living abroad. I wanted home sweet home. Breakfast in bed, the seamless appearance of hot food on the table and sunshine. No beautiful house by the Thames, no red convertible, no amount of shopping or connoisseur Conran's restaurants could hold me back. I came back to Delhi suffering a terrible homesickness.

DIET #24 ● AGE 29 ● WEIGHT 88 KG

DR MCSLIM (ROUND 1)

I was back in Delhi, living in my parents' house, reconnecting with my social circle and taking it easy. This was good for my emotional balance and showed me just how imbalanced my body was. I decided to get onto the diet of the day.

Dr McSlim was, in his heyday, the diet god of Delhi. He was hot in the dietary circles and featured on the speed dial of every worthy mobile phone. A friend's friend gave me his number. She was at her social zenith, newly married and with the perfect home, parties and life. She told us lesser domestic goddesses, 'Always look your best for your husband, girls.' Since then she has been twice divorced. But the advice was good.

I walked into Dr McSlim's clinic and was greeted by two young girls with dark, oiled hair and fresh flowers. They constantly whispered into each other's ears and seemed to have a language of their own. They took my measurements and announced them for the entire waiting room to hear. 'Chast 46, Waste 40, Stomach 46, Haps 56…' And so it went. One announced like the town crier my unseemly vital statistics, the other wrote them down on a thin strip of paper.

The waiting room was the Hall of Shame. Clever tactic, really. Every week you prayed like hell that the Hall of Shame would be empty and you would not suffer the barb of inches. With the ticket of humiliation in hand, more pleasures awaited inside the doctor's inner chambers.

Dr McSlim was lean and shiny-faced, with amazing skin. He looked a little like Mr Burn, Homer Simpson's boss. He took the strip of paper and asked me to climb onto his scales. The scales were not electronic. They had iron weights. He took my weight and speed-typed my humiliation into some MS-DOS program on his computer. It was quirky, to say the least. He asked me what my favourite food was.

'Rajma-chawal,' I told him.

He said, 'Okay then, diet sorted.'

He went on to tell me some amazing things about weight loss I had never heard or read before.

Dr McSlim Nugget #1
Wake up as late as possible so that you can delay breakfast. The logic is that you can cut out a meal by delaying the time you wake up. The earlier you wake up, the longer the day and the more calories you have to feed your body.

Dr McSlim Nugget #2
Minimum fruit. Fruit is not good for you. Too many calories. No fruit juice ever.

Dr McSlim Nugget #3
Don't eat at the table. Serve yourself in bowls and move away from the table. Ideally, eat in front of the TV.

Dr McSlim Nugget #4
Never buy a brick or tub of ice-cream. Buy and eat only the small single serving cup. This way, the quantity is limited and finite.

Dr McSlim Nugget #5
Don't exercise. You are too overweight for it to really make a difference. Exercise will only make you hungrier and fatter.

I found all this absurd and against everything I had learnt about weight loss. But it suited me just fine, so I didn't argue. Many of his radical thoughts have since been proved right. In fact, recent research has shown that the more people exercise, the more they feel they need to reward themselves by eating the wrong food. They believe they have earned it.

Dr McSlim's Diet

WEEK I
Breakfast: Cold coffee made with half a glass of skimmed milk, lots of coffee, lots of ice and froth
Lunch: 2 bowls rice, 2 bowls rajma, I bowl kachumber salad, I cup vanilla ice-cream
Tea: 6 golgappas (made of atta and not suji; they taste no different), I cup tea
Dinner: Any type of dry chicken and salad

It sounded crazy and too good to be true. And if you had been on an unhealthy binge like me, it felt like, Yes! Finally a doctor after my own heart and stomach. Finally, someone who gets me.

Too good to be true

ME   **DOCTOR**

I hate fruit.

                                     It isn't good for you.

I am not hungry in the morning.

                                     Wake up late.

I need something sweet in the afternoon.

                               Have a cup of vanilla ice-cream.

I need rice and with rajma, one bowl is never enough.

                               Eat two bowls of rajma-chawal.

I need something tasty at teatime.

                                   You can eat golgappas.

I hate exercise.

                               Exercising is counterproductive.

I had the doctor's orders to do all the things I wanted to do. I was sceptical because it was a little too good to be true. What was the catch? I followed his diet and his plan for one week. And lo and behold, I was 1 kg down in a week.

I visited him every week. I would hand in my strip and jump onto the scales. And he would ask, shiny, beatific smile in place, 'So, have you been good?' This was confession time. You had to discuss your week's sins and he talked you through them.

He gave me the same diet for two more weeks and then slowly started cutting down. Here was the catch. He started cutting back on the rice and ice-cream but he did it slowly. This was clever because by now I was a little bored of my favourite food and I had tasted the high of losing my first few kilos. I trusted him and was willing to follow him to the end of the earth, or at least to the next meal.

Dr McSlim's Diet

WEEK 4

Breakfast: Cold coffee, made with half a glass of skimmed milk, lots of coffee, lots of ice and froth

Lunch: 1 large bowl of ghiya (bottlegourd) ka raita spiced with a tarka of salt, pepper, roasted cumin, black mustard seeds, curry leaves and whole dried Kashmiri red chilies sautéed in just a bit of oil

Tea: Diet bhelpuri with puffed rice, onions, green chilli, chat masala and lemon, tea

Dinner: 1 bowl vegetable (he chose one vegetable that you had to stick to for the week. Okra and beans were his favourites), 1 roti / Chicken and salad

The raita, I have to say, is his 'killer app'. It keeps the tummy in perfect order because yoghurt and ghiya are both excellent for the tummy and it is very filling. And it sounds yuck but the south Indian spice spike makes it quite tasty.

Dr McSlim Nugget #6
It's not the size of the roti but the number that counts. Some of his clients would make a giant roti equivalent to four rotis but he said that did not count.

Dr McSlim Nugget #7
Eating the same vegetable daily means that you eat less because you get bored of it and the body absorbs less because it gets bored too.

Dr McSlim's Diet

WEEK 6
Breakfast: Cold coffee made with half a glass of skimmed milk, lots of coffee, lots of ice and froth
Lunch: 1 large bowl of ghiya ka raita
Tea: Bhelpuri without the papri and sev but with the aloo and all the chutneys, tea
Dinner: Chicken and salad

Dr McSlim's Express Exercise

After six weeks, he added some exercise. It was very basic but extremely effective. It did not make me break into a sweat or get my heart rate up or make me feel hungry. It needed no equipment. It took six minutes and simply targeted the problem areas. It could be done anywhere, any time and in any clothes. The aim was to rule out excuses like:

Excuse #1: Did not have time to exercise.
Excuse #2: Was not carrying workout clothes.
Excuse #3: Could not get to a gym.
Excuse #4: Was at a meeting.
Excuse #5: Did not have a place to shower.

He introduced exercises 1 and 2 first and slowly added more.

Exercise #1
Stand straight with your back against the wall. Hit your hips against it 100 times. Apparently, this breaks down the cellulite.

Exercise #2
Stand with your shoulder in line with a wall. Place your palm flat on the wall to balance and lift your leg sideways 100 times. Turn around and repeat with the other leg.

Exercise #3

Stand sideways with your palm flat against the wall and swing your leg forward and up and then back. Do this 100 times. Turn around and repeat on the other side.

Exercise #4

Stand sideways with your palm flat against the wall and swing your legs from side to side. Raise to the side and stretch as far as it will go and then cross over. Do this 100 times. Turn around and repeat on the other side.

Exercise #5

When you have only a few kilos left to lose, you are graduated to the super exercise – jumping jacks for three minutes. I was not given jumping jacks. I still had too much weight on me.

Get Yourself a Diet Buddy

A diet buddy is there for you in case of an emergency. For example, if you just can't resist the chocolate mousse. A friend of mine was on the programme with me. Whenever we went out, we either took our own food or ordered our special dietary requirements. Instead of being embarrassing, it became a joke. It also allowed us to keep a tab on each other in social gatherings and laugh at our predicament. Getting a diet buddy is a great idea. A doctor can only do so much; a friend can do much more.

The diet was going really well.

But after a point I got bored and it started feeling restrictive. I got sick of eating raita for lunch and non-vegetarian for dinner every single day. I complained and asked for a change. And I got it.

I am not quite sure how you lose weight on this diet as it defies all logic but trust me, you do.

Dr McSlim's Diet

WEEK 8
Breakfast: Cold coffee, made with half a glass of skimmed milk, lots of coffee, lots of ice and froth
Lunch: I McDonald's aloo tikki burger without cheese
Tea: Tea, any two biscuits of your choice (including chocolate and cream-filled ones)
Dinner: The eternal favourite: raita

Dr McSlim Nugget #8
Eat a high-calorie biscuit that you actually like. If you eat diet biscuits, you are not satisfied and you just end up eating more biscuits.

The secret of the aloo tikki burger diet

The aloo tikki burger diet was unconventional but it worked because Dr McSlim's plan was a low-carbohydrate low-protein diet. If you counted the calories on the plan it was about 1000 calories per day. (A Mac D's burger in India has about 250 calories.) It was a diet lean enough for you to lose weight and it had food options that were satiating. Not your stereotypical boiled vegetables. What he did instead was quantity control and this is why I think the diet worked. He was able to get you to stick to the quantity prescribed because he encouraged you to buy it from the vendor, so there was no leeway in interpretation of size and portion. It also worked because he gave you tasty food so it did not feel like denial. How could you cheat on an aloo tikki burger or on golgappas?

Walk the talk

After I had done the seven-minute workout routine for a few weeks, he asked me to include walking in the plan. Nothing too strenuous, just a gentle walk for twenty minutes. I walked regularly with my diet buddy in Sirifort Park. She was a great influence in getting me there but not the best influence as she usually wanted the walk to be followed by hot jalebis at the Evergreen sweet shop. That aside, it's always good to walk with a friend. Time flies. Sometimes we would be so engrossed in gossiping that we would even forget to count the rounds.

WEIGHT LOST: 15 kg

WISDOM GAINED: Quantity control is more important than quality control.

DIET #25 ● AGE 30 ● WEIGHT 72 KG

MASTER CLEANSE: TRULY A DIE-ET

I chanced upon this diet while editing a news story about women who had lost 10 kg in fourteen days. The thing is, when you are desperate and depressed and you look at these miracle diets, you actually see a light at the end of the tunnel. They promise incredible weight loss in no time, so you make mental calculations and all kinds of compromises – I just have to give up ten days of my life and I will be a size 0 or thereabouts. I just have to give up fourteen days for 10 kg. The gain – or loss, in this case – is worth the sacrifice. Just fourteen days.

I bought the book. It was written in the fifties by a doctor called Stanley Burroughs. The language is old-fashioned and the layout simple. It looked a bit like the free pamphlets given away by religious groups.

I loved the simplicity of this diet. No food, no planning. Just a super drink. It's more a fast than a diet. It has to be followed for a minimum of ten days.

I was supposed to drink the magic potion whenever I was hungry. I could drink 6 to 12 glasses of this drink in one day. The special recipe is just lemon, maple syrup and cayenne pepper. The mix is supposed to be very effective as it has properties that aid detoxification and weight loss and control hunger. Miraculously, it also contains all the nutrients the body needs for fourteen days. The only thing it does not aid is flushing. So you are supposed to take laxatives or do saltwater therapy to aid with the flushing.

Maple syrup is full of nutrients and vitamins; these include iron, chlorine, potassium, calcium, magnesium, manganese, copper, phosphorus, sulphur and silicon, not to mention Vitamins A, B1, B2, B6 and C. Lemon juice is used to produce more bile in the liver, trapping fat molecules and allowing them to be easily secreted. It also helps to decrease your appetite. Cayenne pepper increases metabolism and aids digestion. It is also a good source of Vitamins A, B, C, calcium and potassium. Water, and it must be purified, is excellent for the body. Blah blah blah! It's just a fancy nimbu-pani, really.

I got stocked up. Pure 100 per cent maple syrup. Cayenne pepper. Lemon juice. And water. Well, water I had. And I was set. Almost. The diet said to build an emotional support group before getting onto it to ensure there was somebody to deal with the crankiness. I began the diet. I was so cranky I needed an army to deal with my surliness.

I think I lasted all of twenty-four hours on this one. And everybody heaved a collective sigh of relief.

But that's the thing about crash diets – the effect does not last. In fact, several years later, the diet came back in fashion because the famous R&B singer Beyonce did it, to get in shape for the movie *Dreamgirls*. It came to be known as the Lemonade Diet. The single-point agenda of these crash diets is to make you lose weight. The moment you start eating again, you put the weight back on. I would add this to my diet as a detoxing drink but not as a substitute for a meal. I have thought about doing it as a day detox occasionally but luckily for the people around me, the thought has not progressed any further.

Lemonade Diet

Drink the detox lemonade as many times as you like through the day

`RECIPE`
2 tbsp fresh **lemon juice**
2 tbsp rich **maple syrup**
1/10 tsp **cayenne pepper powder** – or to taste (as much as you can stand)
250 ml pure **water**

Mix all the ingredients in a large glass.

WEIGHT LOST:
None except that equivalent to temporary mind loss

WEIGHT GAINED:
None except that equivalent to a massive headache

WISDOM GAINED:
Beyonce is a goddess not because she sings and looks like one but because she could sustain this diet for fourteen days.

WORKOUT #26 ● AGE 30 ● WEIGHT 80 KG

COLONEL HARD KAUR

I joined my family business and began to put my internet diploma and London experience to better use. I started working all hours and no longer had the luxury of time. I was so embedded in my new job that after a while it was no longer a sabbatical but a move back to India, suitcases and husband not included. My marriage became a long-distance one with monthly visits. Gone was my homesickness. I got back into the full swing of work and I loved it.

My husband moved back to be with me, initially as a trial as he had never lived in India. But then his business took off and he and his business partner decided to shift their base to India. Now I had it all – my life, my friends, bed tea, sunshine and lots of love.

But all was not well. The dietary control was lost. I was starting to put on weight again. Dr McSlim's hard work soon went down the drain. I needed a new plan and I found Colonel Hard Kaur. He was a big guy. He rode a big car. He was tough. He looked like your typical bootcamp trainer. He was strict and very punctual. He came highly recommended. He had fought in many a Fatistan and had won every battle.

His specialty was kickboxing. The workout was intense but I loved it. I really enjoyed punching and kicking. I would take out all my frustration on the pads. He also made me do squats and lunges. His two killer moves were squat thrusts and mountain climbing. They are super exercises with equal measures of pain and gain. The squat thrust is when you squat and then push your legs back into a pushup position, bring them back, and repeat. Mountain climbing is when you go into a plank and then bring alternate knees up to your shoulder.

But three times a week of this was not enough. I got fitter but not thinner. If it's any compensation, I didn't get any fatter either.

Squat Thrust	**Mountain Climbing**

But my diet was not monitored and I pretty much ate what I liked. Meanwhile, work was out of control, I was nearing 90 kg and I was in serious trouble. That's when family intervention was sought. And I was enrolled in another programme.

WEIGHT LOST:
Nil

WEIGHT GAINED:
Nil

WISDOM GAINED:
Diet is far more important than exercise.

DIET #27 ● AGE 32 ● WEIGHT 86 KG

STARVING IN STYLE

Dr Calm's farm was a toned down, politically correct version of Old Mac Hitler's Farm. It was a holistic healing centre on the outskirts of Bangalore, which used techniques and principles from Ayurveda, homeopathy, naturopathy and a wide range of complementary therapies such as yoga, acupuncture, reflexology and acupressure.

The centrepin of the entire operation was the founder-owner-manager-head doctor. He was a holistic practitioner with courses and degrees in all kinds of medicine and alternative therapies and also a qualified homeopath. His wife was a nutritionist. Together, they made the perfect team. Their aim was holistic well-being.

They determined your dosha (Ayurvedic mind and body type) and developed a customized plan, including a diet, Ayurvedic and naturopathy treatments, yoga exercises and some homeopathic medicine. It was a pure vegetarian facility that grew most of its vegetables and it believed in unplugging you from the real world. It was a calm-down, slow-down, destress haven.

They softened the blow of starvation with the addition of luxury and the subtraction of Nazi ideas. No Nazi marches, sirens or raids here. Unlike the jail farm, you were allowed to come and go as you please, though you were discouraged from doing so. It was an oasis of calm except for the minor irritation of a railway track next door. It was spread across a few acres. There was a walking track along the boundary of the property. The rooms were spread around a central garden with thick Mexican grass. I walked barefoot on the soft grass daily; I found it rather therapeutic. The rooms were big, though somewhat bare, and all came with their own private garden, which I might have stepped into once.

At the time I was heading an afternoon newspaper. I was stressed out, I was doing night shifts and my weight was all over the place. I had to destress and de-weight. I had opted for their three-week detox programme. There was no TV or internet connection in the rooms. BlackBerrys and dongles were not yet the norm. Not to be deterred by such minor details, I carried my own fax machine. It took up half my suitcase. I spent the first three days complaining about the lack of connectivity and the useless infrastructure. I brought the place down. I was obnoxious to the management and bristly with the staff. Just like your typical hyper, burnt-out, stressed-out urbanite. By day three they had reached the G spot of my nerve centre. I was unplugged and flopped down like a rag doll. Everything was dreamlike and I felt like I was floating. So, how did they do it?

Unplug

The first step was a detailed session with Dr Calm during which he determined my dosha according to the Ayurvedic system of medicine. The session was gruelling and deeply personal. He asked many questions to understand me and my personality, so that he could typecast me within his framework and into one of the three doshas. This done, I was put on a customized detox and destress programme, including a food and treatment plan based on my dosha and my problems.

My food plan was a juices-only diet. Any kind and as much as I wanted. The day was full of treatments and therapies that suppressed hunger and kept me distracted. The Ayurvedic treatments tired me out and made me numb. Thankfully, the treatments did not include industrial hoses. Some were hard and not so pleasurable but they were balanced with others that were extremely pampering. The idea was to spoil you in ways other than food and make up for some of the denial you suffered in food with spa treatments.

A typical day at Calm Farm

The day began at whatever time you liked but they encouraged you to be in the dining room by nine. The food was simple Indian vegetarian unless you were on detox, in which case you only drank juice. After a sumptuous breakfast of apple juice, I was led to the treatment room for a cellulite-shifting massage. Two women massaged me to a pulp, Kerala-style, with a mixture of oil and dark herbs and granules of sugar that scrubbed and scratched the cellulite out of their stubbornness. The massage was called Udvartanam and it was vigorous. It's an Ayurvedic treatment that helps with overall toning and controls obesity. I was wrapped in a warm towel and made to take steam to let the herbs seep in.

The Ayurvedic steam contraption was quite a gadget. Your head stuck out of a box and the rest of you was inside, getting steamed up. Something like the trick boxes magicians use. This was followed by Shirodhara where they poured warm medicated oil in a continuous stream on your forehead. This was meant to relax the nervous system and open your third eye, releasing deep-seated emotions. For someone as hyper as me, the dripping effect was torture. I could not bear the slow rhythm. I just wanted to pour the pot over my head at one go and get on with it. But calming me down was part of the treatment. It took me about two hours to get the smelly oil out of my head and body.

This entire routine lasted till lunch. I was so tired, all I wanted was to down my juice and crash into bed.

But there is no rest for the fat. After lunch, they let me retire to my room but sent me a herbal mud pack. A wet towel was slapped onto my tummy and 5 kg of cold mud was overturned on it to curb hunger and stop the growling. I felt trapped but thirty seconds later I was in a stupor.

I was encouraged to take a nap. I needed no encouragement. My nap was almost always cut short by a phone call informing me that I was running late for my next treatment. Reflexology. This was one of my favourites. It was dreamology. The pressure points helped with the stress and back pain and they were relaxing and dreamy. This was usually followed by a second treatment, like a facepack or acupuncture. By the time I emerged from the treatment centre, I was ready for some tea and reflection.

I walked around the boundary track and chatted with the other patients. Dinner was at seven and after some more dinner conversation I retired to my room to read and listen to the radio and then pass out till the next morning.

After a few days, I was advised to add yoga to my routine and one of the doctors had a session with me, taking me through the yoga postures that worked best for my body.

Detoxifying and distracting

Their technique of detoxifying and distracting worked. Further, I was not denied on all fronts. If I was denied food, I was also spoilt with wonderful massages and treatments that revived me and gave me a high almost as good as dark chocolate.

Deep heart counselling

Through the week, Dr Calm called me in for evening chats and deep, soulful counselling sessions ensued.

He told me a very interesting fact. When you put on weight, your body becomes sluggish and so does everything else. You put on fat, not just on your body but also on your mind. Your physical, emotional and mental functions, your ambition, sex drive and brain, all slow down. Nobody had ever told me anything about the brain becoming lethargic with fat.

I discovered that the slowing down of the brain and the fact that it could no longer perform at peak level was what was causing me stress. I wanted to work and multitask at the same pace as I used to and I couldn't. The frustration was making me stressed. And because I could not cope, I always felt like I had too much going on. It wasn't that I had too much going on, it's just that the more there was of me, the less I could do. This was creating a vicious cycle. Stress. Eat. Slow down. More stress. Eat. More slow down. More stress.

But now things started to fall in place. He was the first person to describe exactly what I was feeling. I was living life at a lower level. I had shifted gears for the worse. The weight could be seen on my ankles. He pressed my ankles with his fingers and his fingerprints remained. He said it was a symptom of water retention. Water was collecting in my ankles and weighing me down. The body was resorting to its natural survival techniques. It was slowly winding down to accommodate the extra work it had to do to support the extra weight. The body wants to be healthy but if there is no harmony between body and mind, it switches to a lower mode at which it can function comfortably.

This scared me. I was slowly dying at the age of thirty-two. My body was packing up. Unless I drastically altered my lifestyle, I would be unable to perform normal activities.

Dr Calm was a genius at counselling. Through the sessions he unearthed another deep-seated fear I had. I had buried it so deep I didn't even know it was governing my decisions till it surfaced in one of our sessions. I hated kids. I was always the one complaining about noisy kids in planes, cinemas and restaurants, the 'children should not be seen or heard' variety. I had been married eight years and we had not considered having children. It turned out I was scared of putting on even more weight during my pregnancy. And though we had never discussed it, my husband was probably afraid of the same. Dr Calm told me that a woman's body is designed to reproduce and it is the healthiest thing for it to do. He told me having a baby would rehaul my whole system and give me a second chance to put everything in order.

The silent killer

The thought that my body was shutting down because of my weight was what finally shocked me into a healthier routine. I was not ready to call it quits.

I met another patient at the farm and we became friends. He weighed 250 kg. He could barely walk. His knees could not take the weight. He could not drive. He could not even fit behind the steering wheel. His neck had put on so much weight that it pressed down on his vocal cords and it was difficult to understand what he said. He lived in Bangalore and never left his house except to go to his office one floor down. He took the lift.

He came to Calm Farm as a last resort. The first week, he could not make it from his room to the treatment room, a distance of barely thirty metres. By the second week, he could do it with a break. In that one week he lost 10 kg.

He followed the system for a while, but then he started smuggling in food and bottles of champagne. Wonderful as it was to giggle into the wee hours at our little naughtiness, he was too far gone. We checked out at the same time and stayed in touch. He had a heart attack and ultimately died because he was overweight. The medical facilities could not cope with the weight. The ambulance could not move his bulk. The ER did not have adequate equipment to give him first-aid fast enough. They could not jumpstart his heart because the electric current could not travel past the layers of fat. When they buried him, they needed a crane and a special casket.

It was a sad wake-up call. Goodbye, my dear friend, I write this in your memory so that no one has to suffer like you did. Such a wonderful spirit in such a useless body.

WEIGHT LOST:
8–9 kg

WISDOM GAINED:

Fat affects everything. It seeps into the unlikeliest places like your feet and brain. It slows you down kilo by kilo with the ultimate aim of making you completely inert.

5

YUMMY MUMMY WITH A TUMMY

Being pregnant is the best excuse for being overweight. But it doesn't last for ever and soon all the yummy mummies were back in their figure-hugging juicy couture velour tracks. And I? Well, I was just juicy.

THE PREGNANCY DIET

Soon after coming back from Calm Farm, my body rejected chocolate. My body wanted fruit, vegetables and milk instead. That's when I knew something strange was happening. And I realized I was pregnant. My body reacted wonderfully. It immediately gave up all the things I loved which were bad for me.

The first couple of months, I was horribly sick and lost weight. Yes, losing weight was definitely one of the perks. But throwing up on hotel porches while waiting for the car, rushing to use dirty cinema toilets and running out of restaurants to make it to safe ground are not much fun.

Then, like a switch goes off, the day I completed twelve weeks, I was in the pink of health. I was walking, swimming and working. In fact, I was swimming till the very last day.

Mothers-to-be tea

One of the biggest perks of being pregnant was that when people said, 'So, when are you expecting?' I could give a date rather than sheepishly look away and say, 'I am not pregnant, just fat' or aggressively counter, 'Expecting what?'

The second perk was guilt-free eating. I was feeding the baby inside. A baby the size of a kidney bean needed all the cake, samosas and millefeuille I was eating. I invented something called the mothers' tea. It was one big eating fest. A few of my pregnant friends would come over and we would indulge in a table full of goodies chased by glasses of milk. Rather like a bachelorette party, really. There was a feasting table laden with food – there was lemon cake, Arabic walnut and honey cake, chocolate pastries, chutney sandwiches, samosas, biscuits and more. I would order a 1 kg cake for the four of us. We were a gang, united by our indulgent teas.

I'm not fat, I'm pregnant (finally!)

My body never looked pregnant. Not till the eighth month. Largely because I had looked pregnant for so long. My stomach was just as big as before, only the shape had altered slightly. The fat just got redistributed. All my clothes fit because they were maternity size anyway. My walk was already that of a pregnant woman. People had been asking for a few years, 'Are you having twins?' So I could get away without telling anyone I was pregnant. And I did. I never told anyone at work till I was seven months' pregnant. I didn't tell anyone because I was so vociferous about hating kids. I was always complaining about mothers who had children and could not focus on work and now I was pregnant. Sadly, nobody even suspected. They just thought I had piled on a couple more kilos. I think some of the other board members found it strange that I had replaced my espresso with tall glasses of milk but they let it pass.

My doctor said I should not put on any weight during my pregnancy. It would not be healthy for me or the baby. She had to put me on special medication to counter the weight issues. And she was worried about the delivery. During the ultrasounds the doctor complained that the scans were not very clear because the machine had to go through so many layers of fat. Even my gynie was not pleased with the tyres. She could not hear the heartbeat of the baby because it was buried under the fat. This was a little disheartening because the other mummies could hear their baby's heartbeat just by getting their husbands to place their ears on their tummy. Even the baby kicks took longer to be felt.

The first few days after the baby was born, I felt like a goddess except for the pipe from my stomach that was collecting the waste fluids. I looked at myself in the bathroom mirror. I had huge lactating breasts which stood pert and firm and all the layers and tyres had gone. Of course, this was a totally temporary and painful situation, as I discovered later. I was no Greek Goddess, it was engorgement. OUCH! After the baby, following Indian tradition, I was placed under house arrest for forty days. Now I was truly feeding the baby.

Panjiri Laddoo Diet

Early morning: Small cup of milk with Lactonic (a herbal lactating supplement)
Morning: Tea with a highly-loaded homemade panjiri laddoo
Mid-morning: Hot daliya with cashewnuts, raisins and almonds
Three-quarter morning: Apple pie sent over by my masi, eaten hot with cream
Lunch: Rice, yellow dal, kaddu (pumpkin) sabzi
Tea party 1: Visitors. Mothers-to-be tea menu with cakes and savouries and other hot additions
Tea party 2: More visitors, more tea
Dinner: Rice, dal, sabzi
Nightcap: Lactonic with milk and panjiri laddoo

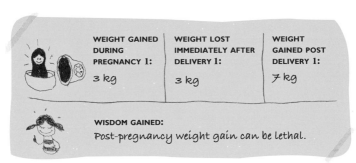

WEIGHT GAINED DURING PREGNANCY 1:	WEIGHT LOST IMMEDIATELY AFTER DELIVERY 1:	WEIGHT GAINED POST DELIVERY 1:
3 kg	3 kg	7 kg

WISDOM GAINED:
Post-pregnancy weight gain can be lethal.

DIET #28 (again) ● AGE 35 ● WEIGHT 97 KG

TWO AND A HALF YEARS OF BEING PREGNANT

The panjiri laddoo diet gave great health to the baby and even better health to the mother! I was really overweight now. My back was giving me trouble with all the extra weight and I found it hard to do anything with the baby.

Six months after the baby, it was time to reclaim my life. I was moving towards this when I discovered I was pregnant again. All plans to exercise and diet were shelved. But this time round, things were different. There were no companion mothers and time just flew by looking after baby number one. But it was a long haul.

Baby number two arrived without fuss. And I was sucked into managing two kids under the age of two, which is agony and ecstasy rolled into one. It's a bit like being in your own warped time and space zone. You are constantly changing diapers and burping and putting one or the other to sleep. I was a walking-talking-feeding machine – feeding the babies and feeding myself.

My weight was once again out of control. The panjiri laddoo diet started again. This time it had the welcome addition of cupcakes. We sent out baskets of mini cupcakes and cheesecakes as announcement gifts for baby number two. Beautiful pieces of pink heaven wrapped individually with pretty pink bows and placed on top of pink checked napkins in little pink cane baskets. There were different flavours like pound cupcake with vanilla icing topped with a sugar butterfly, Oreo cheesecake, raspberry and white chocolate cheesecake. Needless to say, there were baskets where the addresses were not found or the recipients were not home. These were all returned to the sender, me, and kept for home consumption.

We had a new movie projector and were watching episodes of *Lost* on a huge screen late into the night. At every twist and turn I made a visit to the kitchen to get a mini cupcake or cheesecake. And 'mini' does not mean fewer calories, it just means I ate more because they were only mini.

The mothers-to-be tea was extended to celebrate the babies' monthly birthdays. This was just another excuse to eat cake and feast with friends.

By the time baby number two was about nine months old, things had become seriously fat. The scale was touching triple digits. I spent a few months in denial about the scale's verdict. I was embarrassed, my back was in agony and overall I was not in a good place. And I dealt with it the only way I knew – by bingeing.

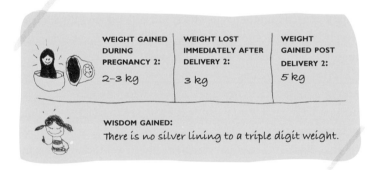

	WEIGHT GAINED DURING PREGNANCY 2:	WEIGHT LOST IMMEDIATELY AFTER DELIVERY 2:	WEIGHT GAINED POST DELIVERY 2:
	2–3 kg	3 kg	5 kg

WISDOM GAINED:
There is no silver lining to a triple digit weight.

THE PYJAMA PARTY AND THE WAKE-UP CALL

I felt like I had been pregnant for two years, which in a way I had. The two pregnancies were so close together, it felt like one long pregnancy. But now it was finally over. Both babies were healthy and bouncing about happily and, unfortunately, so was their mother. And bouncing was not the effect I had been looking for.

Nothing in my cupboard fit and I looked as if I was still pregnant several months after delivery. It was no fun going out. So I just stopped. I was too tired, or it was too boring, or too social. I went into hibernation. Every night was a night in with PJs, soap operas and cake. I must have seen every major American TV soap ever made in those days.

The wake-up call was the kids. I could not keep up with them. I got tired looking after them and that made me cranky and not very pleasant. My back hurt and I could not pick up the babies or sit on the floor with them. I had no energy, my body was going into a state of inertia.

This was not my life. At least, not the way I saw it. I wanted to be fit for my babies. To be able to play with them, run with them, tell them stories and be full of beans. I wanted them to grow up with a happy, cheerful mother, one who stood at the door with a tray of freshly baked pink cupcakes and an apron tied around her twenty-four-inch waist because she herself never ate them.

When baby number one joined pre-school, all the yummy mummies were there in their size zero designer jeans. This was not good. I did not want my little baby to be identified as the child of that fat mother.

That did it. As a mother, you instinctively want what is best for your child. And the way I saw it, at 103 kg I was not the best for my children.

6

FOUR DIETICIANS AND A FUNERAL

Thirty-five years and 103 kg later, I was finally on the right track and I was there to stay. It was not easy, though when I look back, it does not seem that hard either. But it took an iron will and the expertise of many to get there. Together, we celebrated the funeral of the obese person.

TRANSFORMATION

There is a famous fable about transformation – *The Ugly Duckling*. An ugly duckling changes into a beautiful swan. When she is an ugly duckling, everyone shuns her. She is lonely and sad. But then she becomes a beautiful swan and everyone loves her and wants to be her friend. Fairytales are gruesome and politically incorrect but it's the stuff we grow up on. It's hardwired into you: fat and unattractive is unpopular; thin and beautiful is popular. But once you lose more than 20 kg, it's no longer a change like that of the ugly duckling to a swan; it's a whole transformation. A metamorphosis. Transformation of this nature is akin to that of a caterpillar into a butterfly.

The transformation is not just about looking different. It's about living different. The butterfly and the caterpillar lead two separate lives. One is delicate, graceful and beautiful. The other is fat, fuzzy and clumsy. One flits and flies. The other crawls. One just sips nectar. The other eats anything it can find. Losing 45 kg is like that. It created a whole new me. Today, people often ask, 'Hey, where did you leave the rest of you?' They don't realize how close to the truth they are.

I went from a triple-digit weight to 58 kg. I have lost 45 kg and am still counting. I am amazed at the things that have gone smaller and leaner. There are the obvious body parts – tummy, hips, thighs; the harder bits like the arms and calves; and the far too easy bit, the bust. Then there are the less obvious parts like the neck, fingers, feet. I am ten dress sizes smaller, from a size 18 to a size 8.

I have lost weight in other places too, in the odd places where the fat seeps in and you don't even know it. Fat is a silent killer, depositing itself around you, making you lethargic and slow and inefficient. Fat is infectious, so your mind starts losing its edge too. It becomes lazy like the body it resides in. My mind is sharp and all there and I am a multitasking goddess.

DIET #29 • AGE 35 • WEIGHT 103 KG
DR MCSLIM (ROUND 2)

I had done Dr McSlim's diet with great results the first time but had of course yo-yo'd back over the years. Now, at over 100 kg, I needed a solution. I chose Dr McSlim because his diets were initially easy and I needed a kickstart. Besides, I was in no state or shape to exercise or starve. The old diet returned. It almost felt nostalgic.

By round 2 Dr McSlim had become very big. You had to use pull to get in and he was consulting overseas by phone and e-mail. There was a waiting list and I only got in through a colleague of mine who was a regular client and because I was a returning client. Repeat offenders got special privileges.

Back were the atta golgappas, aloo tikki burgers, rajma-chawal and ghiya ka raita.

He never gave you fruit. He never asked you to exercise. He gave you tasty, fatty food. A friend of mine, who was overweight and desperately trying to get pregnant, was doing his diet by phone and e-mail from Australia. He gave her mutton roganjosh for dinner every day because that was her favourite dish and she could order it from the local restaurant as takeaway. She followed the diet and she lost weight. There were no powders or shakes, no machines. Just a controlled diet and gentle exercise.

I never really understood his principles and I didn't agree with them but he made me lose weight and he made me do it without too much heartache. He was flexible and worked with your limitations. Anybody would appreciate that and I certainly did when I met my next dietician.

I did Dr McSlim's diet for four weeks and the scale moved away from the horrible hundred. A triple-digit weight is pretty scary. If you convert it into pounds it's even more shocking – 208 pounds. Especially if most of your friends are half that weight. There was no getting away from the fact that I was obese. But I tired of Dr McSlim's diet quicker than the first time. This did not feel like a life-changing diet. And I was ready to change my life.

WEIGHT LOST:
5 kg

WISDOM GAINED:
Diets work in mysterious ways.

DIET #30 ● AGE 35 ● WEIGHT 99 KG
DOMINATRIX DIETICIAN

I had heard about this bitch of a dietician who was a magician in disguise. Whoever went to her lost tons of weight.

My first encounter was a revelation. I arrived at the grungy basement clinic and was escorted through a labyrinth of grungier rooms. Dark, dingy, smelly. The reception was cramped. It was packed with clients in workout gear, eating, sharing stories and complaining about the food. The walls were bare except for a small white board with the menu of the day. Behind the reception was the dietician's room. It was separated from the waiting room by a thin plywood wall. You could hear everything that went on in there and that, I think, was the point. You were frightened before you were even in her presence.

I sat in the waiting room and bumped into one social butterfly after another. All of whom I had questioned in the past about how they were looking so good and had lost so much weight. They had all been mum then. They just said, 'Oh! I am exercising and eating a very light dinner.' Well, their calories were spilt now. They were being bootcamped into shape.

Then out walked the head whip. Short black leather miniskirt, fishnet stockings, knee-high pencil-heeled boots. Cropped top. Dark kohl-rimmed eyes and red lipstick. This was not what I had expected. But after I saw her in action, I knew this was the perfect outfit. All it needed was a black leather whip and a couple of chains. Complete Dominatrix Dietician. This little package was a fire bomb. She had all my hundred kilos shivering.

From then on, she was DD for me.

She told me how busy she was and pointed at the long waiting list and said I needed to pay now but could not start for another couple of weeks due to the rush. After considerable grovelling on my part, she agreed to start with me shortly.

In the first session she just explained her system. With diagrams. She said her basic principle was to keep the metabolic rate high. She would do this by ensuring I ate every hour but also through exercise and therapy. Her therapies doubled the weight loss normally achieved through diet and exercise. Every week there would be a benefit carryover. So, as long as I did not take a break, the multiplier effect would ensure quicker weight loss.

She explained that the body clock works according to the sun. There is a time when it burns maximum calories and a time when it burns minimum calories. When the sun is at its highest point, our body burns the most calories and we should consume our most substantive meal then. Once the sun sets, our body shuts down and we should zip up because nothing gets digested. The body is in an elimination cycle at this time and if we consume food, it remains undigested.

She then proceeded to take my measurements and asked about my weight history and told me to come in the following week to collect my diet and start the programme.

She said she would change my diet every week. She would meet me every day. I had to eat every hour. I had to fill my food diary every minute.

You needed to commit half a day daily to be on her programme. You had to check in, exercise, get your therapy, get your spot massage, do your consultation with her, get your food, and only then were you done. I had not gone back to work at this point and was still on my post-double-pregnancy sabbatical. The timing was perfect.

There was a gym, massage room, treatment beds and a café, all on the same premises. It was a one-stop fat shop.

The Four Pillars of Dominatrix Dietician's Plan for World Domination

1. Diet
2. Therapy
3. Spot massage
4. Exercise

Basic Principles of DDism

- Her diet was low CCQ – low calorie, low carbohydrate and low quantity.
- No dinner. No question of food after six p.m. The earlier you zip up, the better for the diet.
- Timing is everything. When you eat is more important than what you eat.
- No excuse is good enough to break your diet or skip exercise.
- The portions are small. To keep your metabolic rate high, you need to eat often, but bird amounts, just to keep the juices going.

DD's Deadly Diet

This was my first diet. No easy starts here. I was thrown into the deep end. I just wanted Dr McSlim and my rajma-chawal back.

WEEK I

7.30 a.m. I tsp aloe vera juice, I almond *Yes, one.*

8.00 a.m. Half a Weetabix with half a glass of skimmed milk and a spoon of Splenda

Initially, I thought half is too much because I hate Weetabix but after two days of the diet I was craving it.

10.00 a.m. Portion of fruit

11.30 a.m. Salad with fat-free dressing (provided by the clinic)

1.00 p.m. Lunch (provided by the clinic)

2.00 p.m. Portion of fruit

3.00 p.m. Portion of fruit

4.00 p.m. Portion of fruit

In reality, this should be called tasting; 'portion' is an exaggeration.

5.00 p.m. Coffee with skimmed milk / Bikaner diet khakra / channa chat / I Marie biscuit with tea

6.00 p.m. 200 ml soup (no cream and no packet soup) and I slice toast (on oatmeal bread) / I egg-white omelet with vegetables

There was a small, hole-in-the-wall kitchen that left much to be desired in terms of hygiene and safety. The fact that it made lunch for so many people was a miracle. All the recipes were secret and the women who worked in the kitchen were not allowed to talk to the clients. They dished out all kinds of fat-free dishes on disposable plates and were experts at packing lunch for takeaway as well. Many detractors said, 'How can you eat from a kitchen that's so filthy?' I just opened my mind and closed my eyes. The way I saw it, I was doing far unhealthier things by not being on her diet. Besides, I never got sick with her food and I have a pretty sensitive stomach.

So, what's for lunch?

On DD's diet, lunch was the main meal. It was usually some form of roti, vegetables and soup. Even though the food was fat-free and personally supervised by DD, the quantity was carefully controlled.

The roti was made with a specified atta as written on your diet card. The atta was a mix of bran, oats, whole wheat, wheat germ. The roti was small (the size of a six-year-old's fist) and thick and not very tasty. The soup filled half a Styrofoam cup and the accompanying vegetables were about two tablespoons. On special occasions we were given a treat. On Choti Diwali we got gajar ka halwa made with Splenda. One teaspoon. No exaggeration. One client thought it was pickle and ate it with her sabzi!

Lunch was mean but considering it was fat-free, made in industrial proportions and usually cold, it was not all that bad. I loved the rasam days. And the tiramisu days. The tiramisu was so good you had to have 'contacts' and be able to facilitate the system to get it as it was always in short supply. I don't know how they made it but the mousse and cake bits were delicious and both sugar- and fat-free. Normally, sugar-free desserts are very high in fat but that wasn't the case with the stuff made in DD's kitchen.

DD spent many hours perfecting the recipes, which is why they were guarded so closely. There are four basic flavours that our tastebuds recognize and crave – sweet, salty, bitter and sour. I think a lot of her dishes overcompensated for these basic tastes, which explained the high degrees of satisfaction with the lunches she provided.

DD is the only dietician I have met who actually got the fat person's psyche. She understood the nuances of a fat person's brain. She realized that food was a sensory experience. It was as much about the anticipation as the taste. The daily menu on the wall was deceptively appetizing.

Yummy Sample Menu (and the Yucky Reality)

Banarasi Chat Salad
Reality: Slices of cucumber and tomatoes dunked in yoghurt with a few drops of sonth and chat masala and a sprinkling of anardana. No papdi, no aloo.

Punjabi Chole
Reality: Sabzi made out of tomatoes and onion paste, no chickpeas at all.

Chinese Hot and Sour Soup
Reality: A few drops of soya sauce boiled in water and sprinkled with a couple of stray strands of cabbage.

American Pizza
Reality: A tiny fist-sized roti topped with tomato paste and vegetables. Cut into four pizza like slices. No cheese.

Lebanese Fatoush Salad
Reality: Square pieces of lettuce, cucumber, onion with a watered down hummus-like dressing sprinkled with sesame. No pieces of fried bread.

Portion size does matter

The portions were tiny but DD said you were eating all day because you got to munch on fruit. Now, two things: first, her 'all day' literally meant all day, because when the sun went down the mouth zipped up. Second, the portion size of the fruit had me in shock. You had to eat fruit every hour to keep the metabolic rate up but the portions were so small I was afraid my tummy would not realize something had been sent down to it.

A portion of fruit did not mean one apple or one orange. It meant one segment of orange, a slice of green apple, one strawberry, three gooseberries, three jamuns. And – this was by far my favourite – two teaspoons pomegranate. Ten seeds. That's less than the number of letters in the word pomegranate!

She encouraged eating local fruits since imported fruits, according to her, are injected with substances and preservatives that are counter-productive to weight loss. She said all fruits were allowed except bananas and grapes and her favourite was green apple. But if I put melon in my diary she would say, 'Don't eat white melon, it's too sweet.' If I put pear she would say, 'Oh, they are too juicy at the moment, don't eat them. Have citrus fruits.' So I would buy kinnow and then she would say they were too fleshy. And pomegranate, even two teaspoons, she said was not okay for me. She never explained why. So all I was left with were papaya and green apple. And even here she screwed up her nose, saying that the disco variety of papaya was too sweet.

I did not understand this. Surely the calories of the fruit do not depend on how sweet it is. But there it was, and if you were a truly dedicated DD dieter you would taste the fruit, spit it out if it was sweet and look for the blandest, most tasteless fruit.

So, how did I ever socialize?

The truth is, I didn't, not at first. It was very hard for me to go out at night. One, because dinner plans meant I would be sitting at the table drinking Diet Coke and watching everyone else gorge on food. And although this did make me feel holier-than-thou, I had to explain my whole diet, which made others feel guilty. At cocktail parties, the drinks and roaming snacks were too tempting. Just one battered prawn dipped in sweet chilli sauce, one crispy spring roll, one tandoori paneer, one piece of California sushi and it was all over. A single piece would show on DD's scale the next day.

My husband loved me enough not to force me to go out. And he never insisted I have dinner with him. The poor soul ate alone for months. But I guess for him too, the changes were encouraging as he really did not want the 100 kg wife back. He never insisted I lose weight, as that would have ended up in a fight, but he played the supporting role to Oscar perfection while DD remained the real villain.

For two months I did not go out at night. I let my body settle into DD's new regime so that when we finally did go out, I felt full enough not to be tempted by food. Truth be told, the no-dinner dietary rule is definitely restrictive because socializing is more often than not centred around dinner. The best way to avoid temptation is to stay away from it. You have to make sacrifices. And it is a small price to pay. I started meeting friends for coffee instead. I was allowed coffee at six. That was my dinner. It worked perfectly. I only exposed myself to dinners and parties when my mind got stronger, my tummy got smaller and my wardrobe got hotter.

Once the body settles into the new routine your weight loss motivates you and encourages you not to cheat. Your mind-body-soul has to get hooked onto the high of looking good rather than tasting something good. When I started looking and feeling better, I loved going out. The plans were less about dinner and more about showing off my new wardrobe. I would drink one glass of champagne or white wine and would not open my mouth to anything else. Not even to try the best dish in the world. Sometimes I came home late and had fruit or yoghurt.

Once I broke the pattern of late dinner, I felt much better in the morning. I was fresh and hungry and ready for a workout and breakfast. Falling asleep after a late and heavy dinner, I always woke up lazy, nauseous and not hungry for breakfast. I never really knew the reason for this until I met DD. Now I know it's to do with eating at the wrong time.

Go out, don't pig out

What is that threshold when you know you are strong enough to fight temptation? When you go out and don't pig out. This is a complicated equation of original weight, target weight and willpower. But I would safely say 5 to 7 kg is a good amount of weight loss to turn the tables. And if you are 20 kg or more than your ideal weight, 5 kg is not very tough but it is a significant amount of weight loss. And you are motivated to preserve this weight loss. So even when tempted, your brain advises you otherwise and you are able to resist.

DD's Deadly Diet

7.00–7.30 a.m. Methi dana pani (1/4 tsp methi seeds soaked overnight in water)

8.00–8.30 a.m. 150 ml skimmed milk (no sugar) and oatabix / 1 slice wholemeal toast / 1 granola bar

9.30 a.m. Half a fruit

10.30 a.m. Half a fruit

11.00–11.30 a.m. Salad (no oil dressings/no fruits/no corns/no sprouts)

12.00–12.30 p.m. 1 roti with vegetables (no oil and no potatoes)

2.00 p.m. Half a fruit

3.00 p.m. Half a fruit

3.30–4.00 p.m. Tea and 2 oatbran biscuits / 1 khakra

5.00–5.30 p.m. 150 ml skimmed milk

The therapies

The therapy rooms were like dormitories with long rows of beds. On it lay women of all shapes and sizes, diamonds and fat dripping in equal proportion. The room smelled like a toilet and was thick with gossip. Most of the women knew each other socially. It was a great leveller because you might have had your Dior bag lying by your side but you were sleeping on the same stinky beds and your oodles of fat were there for all to see.

The machines looked rather dangerous. They had little nodes that passed electric currents of various kinds:

1. Ascending current: Light, strong, stronger to shock.
2. Arbitrary current: Shock, pinch, pinch, massage, shock, massage, feather touch, pinch.
3. Drill current: Finds a point, drills down, stops. Drills down, stops. Drills down, stops.
4. Shake and stop: Body shaking current, relief. Body shaking current, relief.

You were strapped on with thick black elastic bands. The fattest clients needed two bands to be tied together. The bands were always a little damp, I would like to think with disinfectant but I know better. Sweat. Somebody else's. If you were fussy, the beds were cleaned with a white liquid that looked like Dettol but was probably phenyl. You were given a dirty white towel. Again, if you were fussy they would give you a fresh one.

It was a women-only facility (because men are not stupid enough to put themselves through this) so you dropped your pants and the electric nodes were tied to your fattest bits. Thighs, tummy, hips, arms… and the fun began. Most of the time, they covered your rolls of shame with a towel but if the serial on the little TV on the wall was *Balika Vadhu* they might forget and you would need to shout out.

They also had treatments other than those that passed currents and made you lose inches. There were heat pads to melt or at least loosen the fat; an aloe vera gel that made me feel like my body was on fire; vacuum therapy where a therapist took a suction cup and sucked out the fat. I found the heat pads relaxing after a workout but hated the other two.

Everybody at the clinic loved the therapies and swore by their effectiveness. Me, I remain undecided. I think this is the weakest link in the chain. If it were as easy as applying a cream or strapping yourself to a machine, more of us would be a perfect ten.

The salvation for these chambers of torture was the attached beauty parlour. While you were getting one of these treatments you could also get a leg massage or head massage or have your polish changed or do a facial or threading or get the untortured part of your body waxed. This was a nice perk. You were losing weight, getting pretty and gossiping all at once.

Spot massage

This was a deep-tissue massage with smelly coconut oil on your problem areas. There was a 6 to 10 minute rubdown along your pillow thighs or muffin tummy or flabby arms. If done with full effort, this could be quite painful. And, to be effective, it had to be.

It was done by a trained therapist and invariably there were catfights (fatfights!) about whose turn it was next. I think the spot massages were pretty effective. And easier to endure if you took your own oil.

Exercise

Exercise had to be done on the premises. There was a gym on the third floor. Frankly, just climbing up the stairs to the gym was more exercise than I had done in a year. Each client was given an instructor who supervised the workout and reported back to DD on the calories burnt. There was a register where everything was noted down by the trainer. The trainers pushed you onto the treadmill or cross-trainer for a cardio workout, after which you were made to do a floor routine.

The workouts were tough. Everything ached. My back hurt and I had to go really slow, but go I had to. So I regularly trudged up those stairs and onto those old machines and gradually it got easier. That first month of enforced daily gym routine built exercise into my life. It became a habit. I finally understood what hotbods meant about the exercise high. 'I can't sleep until I have exercised' or 'I am feeling terrible because I have not exercised' or 'Everything is just sitting there because I have not exercised.' What were these guys talking about? Were they aliens? I never got it. Now I do. The high of exercise is unbeatable and once you get hooked, you can't function without it.

Most dieticians don't stress on exercise or, if they do, they don't monitor it. Exercise without monitoring, for those who are not addicted or strong-willed, is of no use at all. It's the combination of exercise and diet-with-a-danda that worked for me. I couldn't get away with telling DD, 'Oh, I walked three rounds of the park.' She would want to know at what speed, the size of the park, and even then she would not be convinced.

Water therapy

DD was very keen on water. She said it was her secret weapon for weight loss because it carried all the fat away. She wanted me to drink one litre of water for every 10 kg I weighed. That was almost ten litres for me when I joined her. I think beyond a certain weight this formula needs modification. This vast quantity of water is not a permanent requirement but it is important when trying to lose weight as it aids the elimination process. It is also a great calorie-less filler for the tummy and helps curb hunger.

This was one of the hardest parts of DD's diet for me. I am a terrible water drinker. I can go a good two days without drinking a full glass of water. I might have endless cups of tea or coffee but I hardly ever drink plain water. I have extremely dry skin and if I had my head screwed on straight I would drink more than the customary eight glasses of water just to keep my skin hydrated. Besides, I work out hard and I work out outdoors. I never drink water during my workout because I get cramps. I don't even like to drink water after my workout. This is a big mistake because working out, that too outdoors, depletes the water content of the body. In the absence of enough water, the body gets confused, and instead of demanding water it starts demanding food.

But I just didn't feel thirsty. DD said nobody feels that thirsty and just like I was working on shrinking the tummy, I had to work on increasing my water capacity. And it was not about being thirsty. I had to drink water constantly. She wanted me to have a bottle of water handy all the time. I told her I travelled quite a bit and went to a lot of meetings and constantly going to the loo was not practical. She said it took time but the frequent visits to the loo would stop as well.

She asked me to drink a minimum of six litres water a day. The motto was: the more you drink, the more you shrink.

I found it hard. I still do. So I sit with a bottle whenever I am at home and straight after my workout and force myself to drink all of it. I constantly sip hot water with a variety of herbal teabags when I am in the office and late at night. The frequent trips to the loo haven't really stopped.

God's gift to fatkind

Besides the four pillars, DD's success was on account of *her* sheer dedication to *your* weight loss.

It's not your weight. It's her challenge.

She took your weight as her personal problem. She remembered every gram lost and she might not remember your name but she would know your weight. I never knew a dietician who cared so much. It hurt her personally if I gained a kilo. Actually, it hurt her if I gained 200 gm! She tolerated no excuses. It was a zero tolerance policy.

Check out these snippets of conversations between her and her Shivering Clients and you will know the secret of why she was so effective.

In Conversation with DD

DD on dinner parties
Shivering Client (SC): But what do I do, I am going to a party.
DD: Don't eat. Get a glass of Diet Coke and linger with it. Or drink soda with lemon.
SC: But people will ask me why I am not eating.
DD: Say you are on a diet and can't eat. People who force you to eat don't want you to look good. Why do you care what they think?
SC: How can I sit there eating nothing?
DD: Eat the compliments. Food is unnecessary.

DD on growling tummies
SC: My tummy is growling and I can't sleep at night.
DD: Good; use the time to do something. Your tummy will settle down to the new routine. Give it time. You won't sleep for two days and then you will on the third day.
SC: I get a headache by six p.m. because of lack of food.
DD: Take a Crocin and drink as much herbal tea as you like.
SC: It's the third day and I still got no sleep.
DD: Hmmm. Let me check your exercise routine. I think you are not

exercising hard enough. If they are giving you a proper workout in the gym and you are following the diet, you should be passing out. I am going to tell them to work you harder.

DD on special occasions

SC: I need to take a few days off. It's my tenth wedding anniversary and we are going on a romantic holiday.

DD: Do you really need to take a holiday now? You are doing so well and it will ruin the programme. Just tell your husband to cancel.

SC: He has already planned it.

DD: Just think how much more romantic it will be when you are your new shape.

SC: It's my sister's wedding so I will be travelling next month.

DD: Oh no, I think you should change the date to three months later. Imagine how good you will look then and your programme will also be complete.

SC: Huh? The date has been set and I can't change it.

DD: Well, I think you should try because it will be so much better.

SC: I am going for a 3-to-6 film today. What option can you give me for dinner?

DD: Why can't you go after six?

SC: It's a kids' film and the entire school group is going with their mothers.

DD: So take your fruit in with you.

SC: It's PVR, they don't allow you to take any food in with you.

DD: Call the manager out and tell him, 'I am on a special diet and I am happy to buy your food but you need to provide me with some healthy options. Do you sell fruit inside?'

SC: I cannot create a scene in the cinema.

DD: Of course you can. I always tell them, 'Fine, don't let me take my fruit in but if my sugar drops and I start foaming you have only yourself to blame.'

DD on work commitments

SC: I have a meeting this afternoon. Can I eat dinner later than six?

DD: No, carry your dinner with you.

SC: It is a little hard to eat an egg at a meeting.
DD: Why? Just take it wrapped in foil.

DD: I can't help you if you keep going away on trips.
SC: I'm not going on vacation. I have to travel on work.
DD: Whatever. Change your line of work then. How can you lose weight with no regular timings?

SC: I have to travel for work and won't be able to follow this routine.
DD: Why do you have to travel?
SC: I am an airhostess.
DD: All the more reason to look good.

DD on lactating mothers
SC: You know I am lactating and I wake up at three a.m. to feed the baby and after that I feel really hungry.
DD: But I have given you a snack. Three almonds.
SC: Yes, but that's not enough.
DD: Well, you could half each almond. That way it will feel like much more.

Daily dose of DD

I had to meet DD every single day. It kept me on track. The easiest way to go off track is one indiscretion. And then you think, I have eaten that piece of chocolate so why not eat another piece? And there will always be those helpful others who will say, 'Now that you have broken the diet, why not break it properly?' You succumb and think that you will make up tomorrow. On a good wicket you will compensate, and on a bad wicket you will just carry on eating. Best-case scenario: you will not gain weight and the scale will be static. Worst-case scenario: you will gain weight and the scale will show it. Both scenarios are unacceptable. With DD, the scale is paid homage to daily and it must move downwards. There is no room for indiscretion. And trust me, even that one cookie will show up as 100 gm on the scale. I have tried every combination of eating and clearing and there is just no fooling the scale.

Spanish Inquisition

Most dieticians ask you to keep a food diary. It is a pain to maintain and most dieters don't bother and most dieticians don't check. But not DD. Every diary was checked daily and marked. It was like doing homework. And it wasn't enough just to fill the diary. You had to write it as soon as you ate. If you went to her at eleven a.m. and your ten a.m. entry was not in the diary, she would give you an earful. This was why she handed out tiny scribble diaries that fit in the smallest designer bags. DD thought of everything.

I used to write my diary in the car. And she would question its authenticity. 'Why is the handwriting so messy? Did you write it in the car?'

So I started writing it once the car was parked. The writing was neat and clean. Then she would question every entry. 'How much apple did you eat?' 'What colour, red or green?' 'Did you peel the skin or not?' For god's sake, it was only an apple. But the inquisition served its purpose. If you had been fibbing about the entries, then in all the questions she asked and in your delayed responses, she caught you out. The brain was already tired with lack of food and overdose of exercise. You almost always got caught.

So I succumbed, and Prada or no Prada, the diary went everywhere and the scribbling began the minute the food was consumed.

Timing is everything

DD was anal about food timings, they were even more important than the food itself. Lunch had to be latest by one and dinner latest by six. If your entry said one-fifteen for lunch, it wasn't good enough. Even a few minutes here and there mattered to her.

SC: Hi, I have been very good.
DD: What have you eaten since morning?
SC: I had papaya.
DD: What time?
SC: At ten.
DD: It's eleven-thirty now. Are you carrying your salad with you?
SC: No, it's in the car.
DD: It has to be with you. No point leaving it in the car. Receptionist number 1, get her a salad now. I need it in one minute.

SC: Hi, this is my diary.
DD: Have you had lunch?
SC: No.
DD: It's thirty seconds past one. You have to eat right now.
SC: But I am talking to you and I have to exercise.
DD: It doesn't matter. Eat now.

She was even stricter about the evening times and as I continued with the programme, the timings for dinner were brought forward little by little. It started with six p.m. Tough, but doable after much whipping and willpower. But after a point it was four p.m. Now that's pretty unreasonable, I think.

DDism is for life

DD was a miracle worker, whip or no whip. Her system worked. I still follow her principles.

No Dinner

The no-dinner rule worked for me. It was just right for my body. It changed my whole outlook. I woke up feeling energetic, not guilty from the previous night's excesses. Nor did I feel acidic, heartburn, gassy, nauseous or get reflux from undigested food eaten late in the night. And I was hungry. I wanted to start my day with a good breakfast. Many of my friends complain that they are not hungry at breakfast. This is the reason. We eat too much too late. We eat late and wake up groggy, feeling uncomfortable in the tummy and not hungry.

Many experts advise against long gaps between meals. If you eat dinner very early, the gap between dinner and breakfast is too long and this can cause permanent damage to the tummy lining. Moreover, the body goes into starvation mode and sugar levels fall. I don't know, it seems to suits me just fine. And once my body got used to not eating dinner, the idea of eating late put me off.

Daily Exercise

DD got me addicted to exercise. Now, if I don't exercise, my body is not tired, my mind is restless, my emotional balance is out of whack and I can't sleep.

WEIGHT LOST:

28 kg

WISDOM GAINED:

If you are short you can never be tall but if you are fat, no matter how fat, you can always be thin.

The Weighing Scale

This is in a tiny cubicle, smaller than a shower cubicle. Actually, it's not even a cubicle. It's a crevice. In it is jammed a giant electronic weighing machine, in front of it is a mirror and behind it is a dirty curtain on a rod.

It is something like a roadside temple built into a crevice because we all prayed before we hopped on. Or a confession box in a church. You went in, pulled the curtain and then confessed to the sins of the previous day.

I would always go on an empty stomach, wear the lightest clothes possible, empty my bladder before leaving the house and just before stepping on the scale. I removed all external items like hairclips, jewellery, rubberband (though honestly, how much can a scrunchie weigh?), made my promises to the lord in Tirupati and then stepped on. You might think this is an exaggeration but, sadly, it isn't. The verdict was then recorded and presented to the living goddess (DD) who waited inside.

Weighing yourself daily and obsessing over every 100 gm can be addictive. I became obsessed with my weight. After years of eating myself into oblivion and staying far away from a weighing scale, I wanted to weigh myself every hour with every possible combination of food, time of day, position of scale and outfit worn.

7

THE FINAL JOURNEY FROM FAT TO THIN

I was no longer technically obese. I had made
the cut to fat by a very slim margin. Now that
I was just fat, I wanted thin.

DELHI MARATHON

Slowly, I started going to work again. My new weight of 75 kg allowed me to cope with a lot more and I started going to the office part-time, working in the digital arm of the media business.

In spite of my weight loss, my back was troubling me. The orthopedic gave me a back-supporting belt with magnetic metal plates so I could exercise with some restrictions. I was ambling along at the gym. Now I needed a new goal. My husband was going to run the full 21 km marathon. Run I couldn't. But walking the dream run sounded doable. I entered myself for the 7 km run and convinced some of my friends to walk it with me.

I began training in the Rose Garden. One loop of the garden is 1.7 km and I had to cover five loops. I set my target as less than one hour. Major powerwalking and power gossiping ensued, and before I knew it, we were doing four rounds in good time. It wasn't easy. My back hurt and the belt dug into my skin but the target kept me going.

I was very nervous on the day of the marathon. I could not sleep all night. I kept telling myself that it was not a race, I had set my own target. The spirit was what counted. But my brain would not listen to logic. It was panicking. So, after downing half a bottle of Bach Rescue Remedy (this is a flower essence reduction to help with anxiety and emotional stress; it is magic in a bottle), I arrived at the venue feeling very calm and pinned on my number. I had never done an organized run so the pinning of numbers and checking out the other participants felt quite exciting. There was a perceptible energy in the air.

I was worried about where I would use the loo, whether I would finish. But I had my friends with me and I was ready. We walked almost 2 km to get to the start point. It was crazy. Did the organizers know I was just about fit enough to walk this? They couldn't add extra kilometres! I was nervous, my mouth was dry and my breath was short. We made it to the start line and began walking. Once we started, I relaxed and began to enjoy myself. We completed the walk in fifty-two minutes, well under an hour. We were delighted. And decided to celebrate with individual mocha mud pies at Big Chill. This is a dessert so sinful and with so many layers of chocolate and goo and sauce that it can be eaten only once a year. Well, it can be eaten daily but *should* be eaten only once a year.

The daily walking kept me fit and with the on-and-off DD programme, I was not putting on weight – but I was not losing any weight either.

WEIGHT LOST: None

WISDOM GAINED: Regular exercise with erratic dieting will only keep your weight constant.

DIET #32 ● AGE 37 ● WEIGHT 79 KG

MY SISTER'S NEVER-ENDING WEDDING

Your sister's wedding is a very good reason to lose weight. At my brother's wedding, I was eight months pregnant and over 100 kg and not exactly at my photogenic best. I could not bear one more wedding where I looked like that.

At my sister's engagement, I was 20 kg thinner than I had been at the last family wedding. I thought I looked great but when I saw the photographs I wanted to cry. My standards were higher now and my body had not kept up. The wedding was two months away and I wanted to lose another 5 or 6 kg before this one. I had lost the same 5 kg with DD at least three times before. I felt my body was not ready to accept a weight less than 80 kg. I kept going down to 75 kg and returning to 79 kg.

Everyone kept telling me how wonderful I looked. At first I believed them, so the motivation to lose more was low. But when I saw the pictures I knew they had all lied. Or maybe they hadn't. Their compliments were relative. 'Compared to what you were before, you look great now.' This was no longer good enough for me. I wanted compliments that were absolute.

So I went back to DD for those 5 kg. This time, the weight did come off but it was harder and slower.

DD's diet and core training

Besides DD's diet, I added the Core Performance Programme by Mark Verstegen to my workout to strengthen my back. My brother and sister-in-law had just returned from Germany where they had learnt the core strengthening exercises. These are a set of exercises that athletes have been doing for many years but which have come in vogue only recently. They work on the muscles that support the spine and the pelvis. The theory is that once the core of the body – the back and abs – are solid and strengthened, the rest of the body can move more efficiently. It gives the body a better sense of balance and makes it less prone to injury. The exercises give great body tone as well. Since my back was still a little vulnerable, I thought this would be a good way to exercise and strengthen my back at the same time.

My entire family was on a fitness drive to look good for the wedding. We had the core performance book in all formats – hardback, paperback, pocket. Every family member needed his or her own copy. Some needed two or three as they exercised in multiple locations. Everyone labelled his copy and made notes in pencil. In the gym at our house there were sometimes four of us working out at a time. We could not work out together because we were all doing our own versions and were at different stages of the core programme, so we just eyed each other with envy and sometimes with pity.

The core training programme really helped strengthen my back. Plus, the exercises were such weird combinations of the familiar and the unfamiliar that they were a lot of fun to do. But it was a real struggle to actually lose weight. I was getting fed up of how much time and effort DD's programme required as I was getting busier with work and kids. Though it worked, and I met my target weight for the wedding, I vowed not to go back to DD. I had had enough. I was ready for freedom.

WEIGHT LOST:
6 kg

WISDOM GAINED:
Every diet has a shelf life.

YO-YO GIRL

The wedding was a food and champagne fest. The party continued weeks after the couple came back from their honeymoon and so did my food honeymoon. I had vowed not to go back to DD but had not come up with an alternative. Meanwhile, the scale was inching back to 80. Those same 4 kg. I had done the trip from 75 to 79 about four times and I was tired of it.

The family physician said my body had found its mean weight. Everybody had one, and mine was 79 to 80 kg. I was not willing to accept this. I saw it as a resting point. The body needed time to adjust to the new weight because I was demanding such a drastic transformation. DD's principles worked but her programme was not helping me any more. I was yo-yoing back and forth, losing and putting on the same 4 kg. My body had developed a resistance. I needed a change. A new outlook to the whole weightloss malarkey.

WEIGHT YO-YO:
Lost 5 kg
Gained 5 kg
Lost 5 kg
Gained 5 kg

WISDOM GAINED:
The body builds resistance to one system. To continuously lose weight the body must be constantly pushed and challenged.

WORKOUT #33 ● AGE 37 ● WEIGHT 79 KG

TWO TRAINERS AND A WEDDING

Luckily for me, one wedding was not enough and my sister was getting married again. To the same man. This was going to be a Christian wedding in France in five months' time. Where there would be no anarkalis or saris to hide the rolls but fitted dresses to showcase them.

I needed to lose more weight and I needed to do it fast. I wanted to be in my sixties for the French wedding. Even 69.5 would do. I just wanted to shift the paradigm. I came to the conclusion that though I worked out daily and dedicated an hour of my day to exercise, I was not getting enough out of it. My back was stronger and I needed to intensify my workout. I needed a trainer.

The search began. I shortlisted two trainers – one Eastern European and the other American Italian.

Power plate power play

The Eastern European trainer, Volga, wanted to train me on the power plate in her studio, which was the size of a dining table. A power plate is a training machine which works on the principle of vibration and getting your small muscles to contract and do the work. You do a series of exercises like squats and lunges, the vibrations from the machine accelerating the impact of the exercises.

I was not convinced about the power plate. I don't think gimmicks work in the long run. They can help you knock off the first few kilos – in my case twenty – but I think you need the good old hard way of losing weight so that you can keep it there. There aren't really any secrets. Eat less, work out more, and voila! The power plate seemed too good to be true. Fifteen minutes were all you needed on the power plate. If it is that easy to lose weight, why are so many Americans still overweight and why is it not the invention of the century?

I tried it for a few minutes and the vibrations felt strange on my back. I was taking no chances. Bed rest would have been disastrous. I decided against it. But please note: I know many bombshells who swear by the power plate. Perhaps if you are not hugely overweight and don't have a back problem, it's the answer. But it wasn't for me. And so the search continued.

You are not a celebrity, get out of here!

I narrowed my search to another celebrity trainer with a waiting list. Wannatella was a cousin's ex-classmate, so I skipped the queue. She was Delhi's most expensive trainer by her own claim. I think she jacked up her rates after training a certain young lady who is the sister of the heir apparent of our country. This young lady was seen sporting tight-fitted knits with curves in all the right places.

Wannatella was not just a trainer. She was a makeover artist. She changed your body shape with a workout and dietary suggestions but also did consultations on makeup and style. She believed that the main goal was to look good rather than be skinny. Her clients were not necessarily super thin but they looked good for their age and body type. I was very eager to meet her.

Our first meeting was mostly an assessment, during which she asked me about my current diet and workout. It took place in her studio, which was in a glorified barsati. It was the middle of summer and extremely hot. She said she liked to work out without any air-conditioning as it kept the muscles warm and prevented injury. The routine involved a cardio workout on a trampoline for about thirty minutes followed by a squat and lunge workout using a gym ball. The trampoline workout was supposedly injury-proof. It caused no harm to the knees or back as there was no impact.

We fixed to do a private session since she only took one morning class and it already had a waiting list of forty. No one had left the class in fifteen years. Apparently, it was so hard to get into her class that even the Fashionista of Delhi was on the waiting list. And if she gave me a spot, the Fashionista would kill her. Of course, this Fashionista had spies placed right outside Wannatella's house watching every new client who joined her morning class. I was fat but I wasn't delusional.

However, I was somewhat obsessed with losing weight at the time, so when she suggested private training sessions at ₹2500 an hour, I jumped. The heat, lack of food and the high-profile clients had got to me. I agreed. That was ₹25,000 for ten sessions. Crazy. I would do three personal training sessions with her in a week and do her prescribed workout the other two days.

She said she was very particular about timings. On day one, I reached her studio well in time, only to find that she was not in workout gear because she had just been picking up a gift. We got onto the trampoline to work out. She then proceeded to conduct the class in jeans and complained about how she was not supposed to be exercising as she had just had her calf varicose veins blasted. Babe, if I wanted to hear about your problems I would not have paid you ₹2500 per class.

The studio was like a sauna. It was four in the afternoon in May. No AC, no fan. We did an aerobic workout for about twenty-five minutes on the trampoline and it was killing me. I should have told her I could not do any more because she kept asking me if I was okay. But I was enjoying myself. Besides, I did not want to disappoint her. Foolishly enough, I wanted to impress her. I pushed myself to the point of feeling faint and finally had to rush to her loo and splash water on my face and neck to cool down and catch my breath. When I came out she was looking very worried. I said I was fine and just needed to get used to the heat as I normally worked out in an air-conditioned gym. She let me catch my breath and then we did some floor work on the trampoline and some work with the gym ball. Workout over, she gave me a printed diet.

It had lots of good, healthy food: nuts, raisins, fruit, milk. It even included dark chocolate because I had told her that was my weakness. I quickly went shopping for the items to start my new diet. I felt revived and on the path to a new me.

The next day, I followed her instructions and did the cross trainer at my own gym for thirty minutes. I had just got off the machine when she called. She said she could not train me any more because she was a 'celebrity trainer'. People came to her for body sculpting and toning and to get rid of the odd inconvenient bump. Her workout was too intensive for me at this stage. I needed to have a stronger back and less weight.

I was confused. This was a personal training class, so wasn't the workout tailored to my level of fitness? She went on to praise herself and said it took a trainer with some gumption to admit that she was worried about my back and could not be sure of protecting it with her workout. Gone was the 'I am the only trainer with American certification' bravado. She suggested I go to a physiotherapist trainer. She was basically saying I was too fat, not celebrity enough and not fit enough to do her workout.

I was crushed. I had thought I was on track. She had just wasted my time. Now I had only four months to get ready for the French wedding. She should have sussed all this out during the assessment rather than after giving me a diet, doing a session, fixing the routine and taking an advance.

When you are trying to lose weight you might put up a brave front but you are delicate and vulnerable inside. A little incident can knock the air out of you and get you back on a vicious cycle. I had thought I was getting there. Now I felt dejected, rejected, depressed. The high from the Delhi Marathon dream run was gone. I didn't start her diet but finished the entire dark chocolate supply I had bought for it in one day.

Low-carb High-protein Diet

The celebrity trainer's diet I never followed but plan to some day
Breakfast: 7 almonds, 1 glass cold coffee/smoothie, half a melon/pomegranate
Snack: 1 hard-boiled egg /1 slice cheese/oatmeal, 1 apple/pear/kiwi/grapes
Lunch: 1 roti, 1 cup raita/chicken, 1 cup salad, 1 cup dal or vegetables
Snack: Trail mix / 2 slices of turkey ham / raw crudités
Dinner: Grilled chicken/grilled fish/omelet/sprouts, salad, 2 squares dark chocolate/jelly/ice lolly

Follow this for six days. Sunday is your free day. Eat what you want. Satisfy all your cravings.

LOST:	WISDOM GAINED:
Confidence	Celebrity trainers are for celebrities and they are as full of stories as their clients.
GAINED:	
Spirit	

WORKOUT #34 ● AGE 37 ● WEIGHT 79 KG

YOGA GAGA

Being dumped by two trainers was not good for my ego or my weight. I was starting to slip into my bad habits again. But I pulled back. I called in reinforcements. I vented and asked everyone I knew for suggestions. My mother came to the rescue. She remembered a friend of hers who had been completely transformed since she started practising yoga. This particular school of yoga was reputed for making size zeros.

I called Ma Yoganic and she was full of good energy. She said she would send me an instructor the next day. But this time I was not going to take chances. I told her I wanted her to be present for the first meeting. We decided to meet at the coffee shop near her house.

I was sitting in the corner having coffee when in walked Ma Yoganic – petite, pretty, all curves, all smiles. She was in her fifties but looked like a little girl. I liked her instantly. Walking behind her like a puppy dog was a tall male model-wannabe. He was big but you could see she was the one in charge. He had broad shoulders and flat abs and a decent shape but no real presence. He didn't say a word, just put his hand on his chin, his elbow on his knee, hunched forward and checked me out silently. I ignored him. We talked about what I needed to work on and we fixed for classes three mornings a week. Then she introduced the bodybuilder sitting next to her as my instructor. I was sceptical.

The yoga trainers I'd known in the past were in their thirties, dark, of average height and average fitness, occasionally hiding a belly under their white kurta-pyjama. They didn't come six-feet-tall, in their twenties, with flat abs and wearing something from Reebok's extra-tight lycra collection. This would be interesting.

Ma Yoganic's form of yoga was unique in that it trained specific body parts, so a different part of the body was tortured at every session. Sometimes organs and muscles I did not even know existed were discovered and tormented.

Years ago, I had met the Big Guru. This was before his workout did wonders for many a Bollywood size zero. His claim to fame was stopping his heartbeat and breath for several minutes at a stretch. Very impressive. It especially wowed women at cocktail parties. Well, I was not stopping my breath any time soon, just getting out of breath a lot.

The main invention of the Big Guru was adding a cardio element to the asanas, especially the surya namaskars, by doing them super fast. That way, you got the benefits of yoga as well as of a cardio workout. The workout was followed by a luxurious session of passive stretching where every body part that had been worked was extended and stretched to take out lactic acid, thus preventing tiredness and fatigue.

When my hotshot instructor walked into my life, I had got rid of my back-supporting belt but my back was still quite fragile. I was wary of him, though I had been told that he was the best trainer they had and that he trained the six-pack BlackBerry politicians. Trainers in India have no certification and the only way to sort the good apples from the bad ones is to test them on yourself. Not the best plan but there is really no option. So, for every asana I was made to do, I asked him, 'Are you sure this is okay for my back?' He hated me and asked Ma Yoganic if she could send someone else to train me. But he stuck it out, and we eventually found a rhythm that worked.

In the first few sessions, I could not do even four surya namaskars. There was no AC or fan nor was music allowed. My body was stiff and just would not listen. My leg would not go where it needed to and my movements were clumsy and unpoetic. When Hotshot did it, it looked smooth and effortless. It was mesmerizing. I wanted that.

But from the very first session, I felt energized. I was bouncing. I never felt like this after a workout. I learnt later that this energy is unique to yoga. Yoga opens up your energy points and works on the body from within.

Slowly my body started opening up. I reached the point where I could do twenty surya namaskars though they were anything but beautiful and flowing. I was told how Mr six-pack BlackBerry politician did a hundred surya namaskars in fifteen minutes and I thought, now that's impossible. But my competitive mind had found its 'motu'.

The story of the motu goes something like this: Once, I was walking with a friend in Nehru Park. We were walking at a decent pace but we could still talk, so we were obviously not pushing ourselves. In front of us was a fat, totally out-of-shape man. His body looked like a sack of potatoes and he was beating us to it. I could not bear it. He just had to be beaten. So off I went, chasing him around the park. I beat him just before the finish line. Not that the poor soul had any idea he was in the race. The joke became, 'Now that she has seen a motu she goes chasing him.' Well, I had my motu now. I wanted to do surya namaskars as many times as the six-pack politician and as fluidly as the hotshot instructor.

After about two weeks of this, I took a long break for the summer to go to Manali. Hotshot told me to practise yoga and increase the number of surya namaskars daily. He said the mountain air would help. On my return I was meant to be able to do fifty. I said of course I would.

Don't you find that on the onset of your holiday you always make promises about how you will eat less and exercise more, but when you get there, the good intentions start to dissolve in endless buffets and too many drinks? My intentions were good. I even took my yoga mat along. But once I got to Manali, it was forgotten. I blame it on the thin mountain air. I did a lot of walking on dry river beds and trekking up hills and other such activities, and zero yoga. But I was amazed at how much fitter, stronger, supple and energetic my body felt in just six sessions. When I returned home I got right back into it.

The goddess dress

Besides, I had a wedding to go to and a dress to wear. I had found the dream dress. Every day, Hotshot was told about the Goddess Dress. It's a slinky number that ties together with one bow and opens the same way and leaves little to the imagination. I showed Hotshot pictures of it and discussed where I needed to lose weight in order to look my best in it. I talked about the dress so much, he told all his fellow instructors about it. I think the entire yoga gang was imagining themselves in the dress. Hotshot was sold on the dress. Every time an exercise set was killing me and I screamed that I could take it no more, he said, 'Okay, but just think about the dress.' And suddenly I got my energy back.

Hotshot never missed a class and he gave me all the extra time I needed. And I played my role to the T. This meant absolutely no bunking. Not a single class. No being late. Waking up even if I felt awful. I did whatever was asked. I ached, I pained, I was bruised but I was in class. This was the point in my life when I finally understood the concept of 'meetha dard'. Sweet pain. At first I thought, yeah, right, pain is pain. But when that pain led to gain, I got it. Athletes talk about the sweet pain of soreness. It's an acquired taste, I agree, but it's delicious. You only push yourself that extra mile if you can see the goal. I could see the dress.

Be smart, not fat

I learnt this from my fit sister. Work on a specific body part at a time. Giselle was not built in a day. Break it down. When I was trying to get fit for my sister's Indian wedding, I really sweated it out to lose weight, and I achieved my goal, but my sister was far more focused and clever about it. She decided to wear lehengas right through so the only part that was going to show was her waist. She used the entire eight weeks to work on that one body part. For that wedding I was not thin enough to apply body sculpting, but the second time round I got smart. I knew my legs would not show, only my arms and waist, so I got Hotshot to work those parts extra hard.

'Dhan ta nan'

When my classes started again, I confessed to Hotshot that I had done no yoga on my holiday.

After much telling off from my hard taskmaster, I got down to the job at hand. I had a dress to wear. So I got onto the scale, got out the measuring tape and set myself – and my trainer – targets. I wanted to be under 70 kg for the wedding. I had two and a half months and 10 kg to lose. It was unrealistic but not impossible. The idea was to reach for the moon and come back with at least a few stars. (Corny, I know, but this is a self-help book!)

I decided to commit to six days a week, giving myself just one day of rest. The surya namaskars were gruelling. My sides would get mixed up. One leg would just not follow orders. My body was in pain. I secretly popped a painkiller every night for the first ten days.

It took some negotiating but I added music and a fan at slow speed to my routine. Yoga with 'top of the Hindi pops' helped distract me from the pain. Surya namaskar was a daily part of my routine and I was pushed into increasing the routine by two every day. Three weeks later, I could do forty-eight surya namaskars to the 'Dhan ta nan' song from *Kaminey*. I agree that Bollywood and yoga are at odds but, hey, whatever works! I was not allowed to stop there. I was taunted by Hotshot into doing it superfast in perfect form and constantly reminded of his 'other' client who could do hundred.

And then, one day, I did it. One hundred. Hotshot had told me that when I could do a hundred surya namaskars I would be thin. His exact words were: 'When you do a hundred you will look like Bebo.' So there was real motivation to get to that number. When I got there I was in shock. Hotshot was in shock. We did it a few more times in the following sessions to ensure it wasn't a fluke. Now I do it as part of my routine. Just like that. Okay, I am officially showing off.

But hundred was not enough. I could do more. I knew it. So I challenged myself and the following week, I hit 150. And then that was not good enough, so the week after, I hit 200. It felt good to hold the all-time record and be used to taunt other clients. I was definitely the new poster girl of Yoganics.

The next target was to do the surya namaskars against the clock. My target was a hundred in less than fifteen minutes.

From Baba to Bebo

At the back of my mind I always had Bebo. I had read that Kareena's secret to size zero was 108 surya namaskars daily. Now, there is nothing in the number 108. It's just a marketing gimmick. You don't get any less or more benefit by doing 107 or 109.

Until I could do it myself, I thought, nice spin. Of course she doesn't do 108. Who has the time and the energy? But after doing it myself, I know it's not pants. It takes about fifteen minutes and you can do it anytime, anywhere. No special equipment required. The trick is to master the movements until they flow automatically. Regular practice commits movement to muscle memory, that's how dancers do it.

What Happens to Me: an SN by SN Account

I often start the routine with a particular emotion – anger, irritation or fatigue – and by the time I complete thirty, I have forgotten all about it. I start thinking, only a little more to get to fifty, the halfway point. Then I tell myself I need to hit seventy. This is the hardest twenty. Once I cross seventy, it just flows. I stop thinking. I start flowing. I go into a zone. At hundred, I feel peace. I feel in harmony. The 'you' I start with is often not the 'you' I end up with hundred surya namaskars later. I truly believe that there is a greater power in this routine, put together hundreds of years ago. It is a dynamic meditation.

Add an extra punch to your surya namaskar

To add further punch to the surya namaskar workout once I had mastered the number, I started to think about one body part each session. For a while, I focused on the arms. While doing all twelve movements of the hundred surya namaskars, I thought only about my arms. That made me automatically start using that body part more. Then I thought about my abs and found myself tightening my abs through the entire routine. Surya namaskar is a whole-body workout but focusing on one area adds extra pressure on that body part.

By doing the asanas at speed, I got the benefit of yoga as well as of a cardio workout. I simultaneously felt the adrenalin rush of a cardio workout, the fitness of asanas and the calming effect of dynamic meditation. I found it the perfect workout.

Thyroid activating postures

Besides surya namaskar, my yoga routine had a lot of thyroid regulating postures and breathing. I don't have a thyroid problem but keeping it in the best working condition can only help. It must have, because I found I did not have an appetite or any cravings. Yoga seemed to regulate all my carnal desires.

Crunches

There is nothing that gets rid of stomach flab like crunches. But I had a lower back problem so Hotshot was quite restricted in the crunches he could make me do. To his credit, he did invent many postures that targeted the tummy and were easy on my back.

There are several variations of the basic crunch or naukasana:

- Lie flat on your back, arms folded behind the head, and bend your legs at the knee. Now crunch your head and knees towards each other as far as they will go and then away until your head and toes both touch the ground.
- Lie on your back, arms folded behind the head, lift your legs ninety degrees and push your hips up using your tummy muscles.

- Lie flat on your back. Raise both legs six inches above the ground. Now raise one leg at ninety degrees to the other and hold for ten counts. Then do the same with the other leg.
- Lie flat on your back. Raise one leg straight and rotate it clockwise. Now do it with the other leg. Repeat the same drill anticlockwise.

Within six months I was doing an average of 500 crunches, more on the days when I concentrated on my abs. In fact, I was so focused on being anywhere else but in my body that I was unaware of the actual number count. Hotshot now tells me we were doing 800 crunches on an abs day. My level of unawareness helped. If I knew I was doing 800 crunches, I would never have done them.

Awareness

Yoga gurus, mine included, harp on about doing things with awareness. Concentrate on the body part you are working on to get the full benefit of the exercise, they say. I say, forget all that, at least in the initial stages when you are trying to get fit. Be unaware. To bear the pain, to push the body beyond its limit, you need to trick the mind. Take it somewhere else, to a happier place where the body is not being tortured, where the muscle is not being beaten, the fat is not being melted. That is the only way I could take my workout to a high intensity. I would just switch off and take my mind to the beach or the mountains, depending on the weather. I was in bliss, not in the basement of hell.

Yoganics move in mysterious ways

During all this yoga, my diet was balanced and healthy but it was not severe. My weight was stuck and not really moving. I complained to Hotshot and when he had no answer, I complained to Ma Yoganic. I told her to give me the magic mantra. Ma Yoganic told me to have patience. She said the weight might not shift for weeks but the message was getting across. That's how it works with yoga. It talks to the body inside and outside. The body is listening. And one day it will understand what you want and the weight will just drop off.

Okay, that sounds crazy. It sounds like the people who think their dogs talk to them. No surya namaskar was talking to me. But I had put myself in their hands, so I waited and waited and waited. And five weeks later, it happened. My body just got it and the weight started coming off at almost half a kg a day. I had changed nothing in my diet and was continuing with Hotshot's six-days-a-week exercise routine. Heck, what do I know, maybe some dogs are like people with tails!

WEIGHT LOST:
10 kg

WISDOM GAINED:
Yoga is not a form of exercise; it is a way of life.

DIET #35 ● AGE 37 ● WEIGHT 79 KG

THE SENSIBLE DIETICIAN

While I continued with Hotshot and the hundred surya namaskars, I also joined Delhi's most sensible dietician, Little Miss Wholesome. She had no magic potions or principles. She just gave you a healthy diet and monitored it. She had her own brand of foods but her diets were not dependent on them. They were just good old-fashioned wholesome diets!

I had done Little Miss Wholesome's programme once before for six weeks with good results. I left her because I got pregnant. But now I needed a sensible diet, something to compensate for the lack of wholesomeness in my previous drastic diets. I wanted to ensure that at this stage my skin, hair and bones weren't adversely affected.

In my first session, they dug out my card from when I had joined her at 97 kg in 2007. She was delighted to see me at 68 kg in 2009. I told her about the dress and said I needed this weight lost through sensible means in a short time. She put me through the motions. Little Miss Wholesome had a long and comprehensive form that I had to fill out, so that she could understand my food issues and then devise a diet to suit my needs. I had to go for a weigh-in and measurements once a week. I was no longer embarrassed about my measurements and would have liked them announced on a loudspeaker for all to hear in Dr McSlim style. But at Little Miss Wholesome's, everything was sensible, serene, quiet and calm. The session was more consultative. I talked to her about any deviations and issues with my diet. She agreed to put me on a no-carb diet for the six-week period.

The worst part about Little Miss Wholesome's consultation was her heavy-duty, high-tech scale which told you what age it thought you were based on your weight, circulation, BMI, etc. Mine came to 62. I was not pleased, especially since I believed I was now fit. If you take nothing else away from this chapter, at least take this: *Do not get on that scale!*

I was in a good place mentally, was exercising regularly and was highly motivated to stay healthy and lose weight. The combination of big danda on the exercise front and mild danda on the diet front worked. This was a reversal of my previous routine where the diet was stricter and the exercise milder. Boils down to the same simple equation of input and output. At my new, lighter weight it was easier to intensify output and be a little lax on the input. With the yoga and this sensible diet, the weight and inches reduced in a reasonable manner every week.

Little Miss Wholesome's Diet

Breakfast: Cold coffee with skimmed milk and without sugar, 1 portion of fruit (1 apple/1 pear/half pomegranate/medium bowl of papaya or melon/1 orange/a small bowl of strawberries)
Mid-morning: Nuts
Lunch: Yoghurt, vegetable, 1 portion of protein (fish/chicken/egg white/tofu/paneer)
Mid-afternoon: Tea
Evening: Yoghurt, papaya, tea or nimbu pani
Calcirol (Vitamin D supplement): one sachet for eleven days

WEIGHT LOST:
8 kg

WISDOM GAINED:
Little Miss Wholesome's goodness was the perfect antidote for Ms Fad Dieter.

DIET #36 ● AGE 37 ● WEIGHT 71 KG

DAHI PAPAYA DIET

I was well on my way to my dream goal but I had two weeks left and I needed that final push. I was 2 kg off target. Hotshot suggested I try their signature dahi papaya diet.

This diet gets full marks for simplicity. For one week you eat dahi and papaya. As much as you like, whenever you like. You are allowed lemon and seasoning. You can eat them together or separately but add nothing else to the diet. You can take the yoghurt in any form, like lassi, as a smoothie or just on its own.

When I told my official dietician, Little Miss Wholesome, that I was doing this diet, she was not pleased but said it was fine as long as I added other fruits and milk and if I did it for three days rather than a week. I was too desperate to listen. I just wanted to shift the scale.

This diet was hard, I shall not lie. A couple of times I cheated with masala tea and on one occasion with a full Chettinad lunch without carbs. After a week of the diet, I felt orange. But both the foods allowed on this diet are so rich in nutrients, my skin glowed. And my tummy felt cleansed and happy. To top it all, I was applying papaya and dahi facepacks on alternate days. This is a home remedy for glowing skin. Of course, I had the extra benefit of being able to lick the stuff off my face, and dinner was done!

As for the results, they were amazing. Three kilos in one week. I called Ma Yoganic and told her how wonderful the diet was and complained that she had not told me about this miracle diet before. In typical yogic speed and tone, I was informed, 'All is revealed when the time is right.'

As the wedding day drew closer, the dress became more and more real and I was still pushing myself hard. I weighed myself the day before I had to travel to Paris. I was 68.5 kg. A whole kilogram less than I had planned. I was delighted. I could not believe it. I had never thought I would hit 69. It was a pie in the sky. But to achieve it rather than eat it felt almost surreal.

I would say this was a major turning point for me. I had set a tough target and I had achieved it. It made me feel like the king of the world. Or queen. It was incredibly empowering. I felt light in body and in spirit. I had new respect for ancient wisdom, for my hotshot trainer and, most importantly, for myself. Something more than my weight had shifted.

Dahi Papaya Diet

Breakfast: Papaya with lemon
Snack: Papaya with lemon
Lunch: Low-fat yoghurt with black sesame seeds, roasted cumin and salt
Snack: Papaya with lemon
Tea: Papaya with lemon
Dinner: Low-fat yoghurt with a south Indian tarka
Nightcap: 1 tbsp yoghurt with roasted cumin
Green tea throughout the day

WEIGHT LOST:
3 kg
WEIGHT KEPT OFF:
3 kg

WISDOM GAINED:
This is an excellent desi concoction for quick weight loss. Side effects include glowing skin and a cleansed tummy.

LIKE WATER FOR CHAMPAGNE

My makeover team (dieticians, trainers, designers) was just as excited as I was. They wanted to see the dress on me now. There was no time to show them the dress before I left for the wedding. France was calling. But it served as motivation to stay on track in France. When I got back from the wedding, I had to still fit into the dress and model it for the team that had helped me get into it in the first place.

The wedding was beautiful. It took place in Annecy, a tiny village next to a lake. Food played a big part in the wedding. Champagne played an even bigger part. My brother-in-law is French. When

Indians get married they take along their family; the French, well, they just bring champagne. We were drinking it like it was water. We would start our morning with champagne and scrambled eggs and the gourmet journey would continue all day till we had a late nightcap with champagne. And then one flute for the road or the lift up to our room. We were practically brushing our teeth with the stuff.

I had been severely deprived for many weeks. And this could potentially have been a big disaster. There was no gradual stabilizing process here. One day I was doing dahi-papaya, the next day I was deep in the land of French pastries, cheese, baguettes, croissants and champagne. Let loose in the wrong country.

But I was surprisingly good. I did my surya namaskar workout daily. This in France, where the hotel rooms are famed for being very, very tiny. I stood in the narrow space between the twin beds and just got on with it. What came over me? Well, I had to still fit into the dress when I got back and things just did not feel right till I had spent 15 to 20 minutes doing yoga. It was hardwired into my system. I was becoming one of them; a yoganic. Or maybe it was the champagne playing tricks with my mind.

This routine also became the germ and gem of an idea for a diet that involves lots and lots of champagne. But more about that later.

WORKOUT #37 ● AGE 37 ● WEIGHT 69 KG
RUNNING AND ROLLING

Wedding over, dress worn. I wanted more. They say you can never be too rich or too thin. They are right. I wanted to weigh in the fifties now. I wanted to lose 10 kg more. I needed a new goal.

There was a general consensus among my many weightloss advisers – some experts, some bystanders, some slouchers – that running was the next logical step. My husband, a marathon runner himself, encouraged me whole-heartedly. I didn't want to do it at first, because I had never run before, but I was overruled on all counts. I had to do it.

I set myself (was forced to set) a target of being able to run a 5 km mini-marathon by the end of the year. That was two months away.

Basement runner to blade runner

I am ashamed to say this but I started running by doing laps in my basement. I have a large basement. A big empty space of 2000 square metres. It became my own track and field stadium.

My face would turn red, I would sweat profusely. On many occasions I thought I was having a heart attack. I would do five laps of the basement and collapse. To put things in perspective, this was roughly 35 metres a lap.

I was then pushed to try my feat outside. Hotshot found a 50-metre stretch in the park. He would sit comfortably on one end of a park bench with a blade of grass in his mouth, eyes closed, legs crossed, as if he was sitting on a charpoy in a village surveying his land. Only the hookah was missing. I would do 100 metres back and forth. I was the cow that was tilling the land.

Slowly I learned to do two rounds and then a little more and a little more. Next I graduated to the Rose Garden circuit (1.7 km). The idea was to do as much of the round as I could running, take a walking breather, and go again. I literally had to be pushed to run. Hotshot (finally off the charpoy) ran behind me with his hand on my back, pushing me and stopping me from collapsing. I found it the hardest thing I ever had to do. Much worse than 200 surya namaskars. I would be out of breath in seconds and the blood would go rushing everywhere, making me dizzy. And there was the relentless whispering of the voice in my head, 'You can't run, you can't run'. But I was not allowed to give up. So on and on we laboured.

'You also beautiful'

One day, a man was doing all kinds of fancy cardio moves in the park while I was being put through my running drill. I noticed that he kept looking at us. As an excuse to take a break from my toil, I started talking to him. He told me he used to be in the national volleyball team and still kept fit with this routine. Hotshot joined us and told me, 'Oye! No breaks! Get a move on.' I introduced Hotshot to my new park friend as my trainer who was helping me get fit.

The national volleyball champion surveyed Hotshot, smiled and said, 'Very good work. You are beautiful.' Hotshot smiled coyly and said, 'Thank you.' Like, what just happened here? Here is me: plump but not half bad-looking and a woman too, and he looks at a strapping six-foot Jat boy and calls him beautiful. The champion looked at me as an afterthought and said, with no conviction and some pity, 'And you also beautiful.' That was it. I was pissed. I was determined not to be the 'you also'. I had found my third 'motu'.

I suffered the daily torture with fortitude. Well, something that appeared to be fortitude. It was on one such screaming-stomping fit that the secret of running was revealed to me.

The secret to running I never knew to ask and was never told

And here it is.

It's breathing through your nose.

You just don't open your mouth. You never, ever breathe through your mouth. The first thing I used to do when I ran was open my mouth and start breathing heavily. And now I know that's the worst thing you can do. It's like blowing out all your reserves and energy.

I had to focus on my breath. Breathe deeply through my nose and keep my mouth sealed. I diverted all my attention to just taking in air and pushing it out and tried to forget everything else. It worked. My legs knew how to run. I did not need to focus on them. And I didn't lose all that extra energy through my mouth. Plus, the focus on breathing silenced the negative voice in my head. And once my breathing fell into a rhythm, my heart followed. It took practice. I didn't get it in one run but I kept at it. I had to bite my lower lip with my teeth on occasion to keep my mouth tightly shut.

Please don't dismiss this theory as too simple. I did at first. But with a personal trainer you don't have much choice, so I had to give it a fair chance. And it worked.

With this revelation, my running distance went up dramatically. Soon, I could do a decent 800 metres, take a mini break and go again. And go I had to because there was Hotshot waiting for me at the end of the line, either hanging from a tree or sitting on a bench eating his customary blade of grass. After I built my stamina with these jogs, I was encouraged to increase the duration. And as the weather cooled down and I got fitter, I was able to do so.

What are you doing, you can't run!

The day I completed half a circuit of the Rose Garden – about 1 km – I was excited. Now I knew the breathing technique was the key. But if I wanted to complete the entire circuit of 1.7 km I would have to break a mental barrier. My mind was shutting my body down, saying, 'You can't do no more'. My mind was too conditioned to the fact that I could not run. First it was my physical body that could not cope and my mind had to push it to try, and now that my body was ready to go, my mind was stopping it. I knew it was just a mental hurdle that I had to cross. I have never believed in motivational books about positive thinking, the power of 'can', the secret laws of attraction, etc. I thought they were for weak people. You know what, they are for the smart. They work. I have not read any books but just applying the philosophy of 'I can' was crucial. I couldn't run around that garden until I believed I could.

The first time I managed to complete the circuit without stopping, I was elated but not convinced. I thought it was a fluke. Only when I had done it successfully a few times did I believe it. After that I started doing laps. My goal was three laps, which is a little more than 5 km.

My own dream run

I started my running routine in September. I took a break all of October and restarted in mid November. In early December I did a 5 km run for the Running and Living Foundation in Gurgaon. It was awesome – awesomely tough. I wanted to stop after the first 100 metres and then every 100 metres thereafter. It was a hot winter's day, the route did not have an ounce of shade and I had too many clothes on. I had never done a 5 km circuit anywhere other than the Rose Garden. I felt like a running virgin. I had no faith in my ability to run the distance anywhere but in the Rose Garden. And even there I could run only in the clockwise direction. Any change in the variable – shoes, music, circuit, gear, direction – and it was a touch-and-go situation.

I had to push myself hard that day, but somehow I made it past the finishing line and past the proud face of Hotshot, who maintained a mask of quiet calm as he informed me that I had completed 5 km in 34 minutes.

After crossing the finishing line, I felt faint, dizzy and nauseous and went and collapsed in the shade of an ambulance with a bottle of water. Slowly, normalcy returned and with it the elation of running 5 km on an unknown circuit with none of the variables in perfect order. The pain is temporary, the joy for ever. That night I went celebrating. Everything was allowed. Champagne. Music. Dancing. Collapsing. I had crossed a major milestone.

I started running at age thirty-six. I wasn't tapping into some earlier talent. I trained and went from running 0 km to 5 km in just six weeks. If I can, anyone can.

What Kept Me Going?

The goal I had set myself. I was not ready to let myself down. I took it very seriously. Everybody said it wasn't a big deal, that I could always try again if I couldn't do it this time. But in my mind there was no next time. You let a goal slip once and it's all too easy to let it slip again. I put a lot of pressure on myself and I told all my friends and family that I was running because I knew they would all ask and I could not bear the thought of saying I had failed.

Born to run

From then on, running became an essential part of my workout. Later that month, I decided to have a party to celebrate my birthday. As a departure from previous birthday feasts, the party was preceded by a run. That's right, major departure. No feasting without fasting, to go with the new me. The new me wasn't about being good every day and then letting loose on my birthday; it was about doing both. I did a morning run in Gurgaon with the

Running and Living Foundation. The run was far easier this time. I was fitter, dressed smarter, and there was a breeze. This was followed by a lazy all-day brunch with bottomless mimosas and much guilt-free eating.

This is definitely one of my magic tricks for weight loss. Running. Obvious? Yes. I think running is the answer to all ills or all fats. But it's a catch 22. In order to run, you need to be fit enough in the first place. If you are obese, you cannot run because you can develop knee and back problems. But if you find a trainer who can build you up slowly, you can.

Now, as I complete my third 5 km Running and Living run, I wonder what my trainer must have thought of me collapsing, running around my basement. And I think about how far I have come. I have now run through pine forests in Manali, on the beach in Goa and up a mountain in Vancouver but sometimes I still wonder whether I will be able to complete that circuit in the Rose Garden.

Tricks to going from 0 to 5 km

- Breathe right. Don't breathe through your mouth. Force it shut by clenching your teeth over your lower lip.
- Listen to music on your Ipod. You are not thinking about running and how hard it is. Your mind has wandered with the music somewhere else.
- Run outdoors. I never run on the treadmill. My entire workout is outside. I find that trees and nature in general are energy boosters. They add another dimension to your workout.
- Don't get a buddy. I can't run with another person. I can't talk. I need to focus on my breathing. I need to keep my own pace.
- Add variety by changing the outdoor venue or type of running.

- Drink lots of water after you finish. I cannot drink while running because I get cramps, but if you can, then drink during and after. Running severely depletes the body fluids and makes you feel hungry. Your body is actually craving fluid rather than food but the signals can be confusing. So before you plan your lunch, make sure you first drink water.

To Gym or not to Gym

Workout in gym. Wait your turn. Finally get your turn on a sweaty treadmill. Wipe it down. Begin your workout. The TV in front is blaring. The music is constantly switching because some don't-you-know-who-I-am wants his favourite playlist played. People are talking loudly on their cellphones. The AC is sort-of-working. Everybody is sweating and smelly. Breathe recycled air. Hot, unpleasant and stressful.

VS

Workout in a park near you. Spacious track. No waiting. Play your own music on your Ipod. See the trees. Smell the freshly cut grass. Hear the birds. Breathe fresh air. Give your mind, body and soul a healthy dose of nature. Get out of your normal routine. Switch off. This is addictive. And you will want a daily fix.

Running uphill

Nothing melts fat like running, and uphill running is the best. I swear by it. It is also a lot of fun. Initially, I found it tough but not tougher than running. Because you can always see the top of the hill and you get to walk down. So you get a break before you start again. Also, running on flat ground feels much easier after this.

I sprint up. I catwalk down or walk down backwards or sideways. I have fun with the downhill. Here too, I focus on different body parts. I find that if I concentrate on my upper and lower tummy, I can actually use those muscles to propel myself forward.

Interval training

This is such a high. You give it all you've got for twenty seconds and then you get to walk leisurely for twenty seconds. I was amazed at the speed I could achieve. As you get fitter, you can increase the time you spend sprinting and reduce the time you spend walking leisurely.

Running is for you and you and you

The thing is, if you have a basic level of fitness, running is not impossible. When I started running, I had a decent level of fitness and a newly recovered back. But if I could do it so late in life, so can you. So don't rubbish it till you have tried it.

There is something pure, almost primate in running. It's as if we were designed to run. Maybe not everyone is a Bolt, but human beings are built to run, to move about – not to sit behind keyboards typing all day or in cars driving and texting. It has a feel-good factor, a rush that's indescribable.

The aha! moment

Running the circuit nonstop without a break and reaching my target weight before the French wedding was my aha! moment. The penny dropped. I was ready to take life head on.

A while ago, I had this recurring dream for several nights. I was running freely and effortlessly in the grass, breeze blowing through my hair. I was 100 kg at the time and I am not sure how this thought even entered my head. But there is something liberating about running. It feels like you can run away from it all or to it all, the choice is yours.

In the park I was pushing my body to a new distance and outside it, I was pushing the envelope with my life. I got back in the driving seat and restarted driving. I started accepting public speaking engagements. I started buying clothes I would never have worn earlier. I started accepting coffee invitations with new people. I entered dream runs. I made new friends. I tried paragliding. I went on holiday by myself. I was looking at the world with new eyes. It was as if breaking one barrier freed my mind from other barriers. I was willing to challenge my boundaries and take things head on. It was like the first day of the rest of my life.

WEIGHT LOST: 10 kg

WISDOM GAINED: Running can free you from the old you.

DIET #38 ● AGE 38 ● WEIGHT 59 KG
THE CHAMPAGNE DIET

Mona: Boss, iska kya karein?
(What should we do with him?)
Ajit: Isko champagne pilla do. Agar ye shame se nahi marega to pain se mar jayega.
(Give him champagne. If he doesn't die of the shame he will die of the pain.)

You have been warned.

All you dieticians and trainers out there are going to cringe when you read this bit but this is a tell-it-like-you-eat-it book. So skip this section please. All you serial dieters: read on.

This diet is unconventional and is rooted not in any wisdom but in lots of experience. And I absolutely love it. It's my very own concoction. And it came about accidentally as all great inventions do. But I tried and tested it. I refined it. And you are getting the absolute Cristal version of it. But I take no responsibility for it other than the fact that I have done it and it works for me. It's the perfect diet for the week you are partying – like a wedding or a long weekend.

Like I told you earlier, my brother-in-law is French. He drinks champagne like the English drink tea. Anytime, anywhere. He would come for tea to the house, it would be the standard chai-samosa-jalebi affair. When I asked what he would like to drink he would look uncomfortable for a moment, look at my sister for reassurance and when she sighed with resignation, he would say, 'Champagne, please!' At four in the afternoon!

For as long as I can remember, our traditional Sunday family lunch has been chicken biryani and parantha, a menu handed down over generations. There have been no aberrations but since the inclusion of a Frenchman in the family, champagne has become an essential addition to the Sunday routine. It is now a family tradition. As a result I have become quite a champagneholic. And that is the origin of this diet.

A typical weekend on the champagne diet

It starts on Friday night. Not on Monday morning. It begins with a glass of champagne. And it ends with a glass of champagne. In between there are, well, many glasses of champagne. Nothing else, not one tiny bite of anything. I focus on the champagne and the poise. And if there is dancing, then on the dancing.

Dancing is the best workout. A friend who had not seen me for a while was complimenting me on my weight loss and asked me to dance. When I started dancing he said, 'Babe, you're not dancing, you are just doing your aerobic workout.' This had not occurred to me before, but how perfect. You sip champagne, you dance, you burn calories and create your own bubbly cycle – what more does a girl want?

Drinking on an empty stomach gives me a quick buzz. Light weight and light headed, I can go longer and party harder. I come home in the wee hours of the morning and crash. I sleep like a baby, no, like a dead person. I need only a few hours because champagne-assisted sleep is so deep I am soon ready to go again.

I open my eyes and even before I can feel the hangover I do kunjal kriya. This is a yoga technique for internal cleansing. It's a bit yuck but it works wonders. It is also a great cure for a hangover.

Kunjal Kriya

You need a jug of lukewarm (easy-to-gulp temperature) water, a glass, a bowl of salt and a spoon. Add a spoon of salt to the glass. Fill it with water and drink quickly. Repeat till you can't drink any more. My limit is about four glasses. By the fifth glass your tummy will start hurting and bulging out. Just let it out. Initially, you may need to use your fingers to force it out. The salt water flushes out the whole system, including all the acid that makes you nauseous.

I am the eager beaver up and fully functioning at nine a.m., sending texts about the great night out. All my friends surface at noon with heavy heads, ready to kill me. And I am ready to go again. One refinement of this diet is that I need two groups of friends. One set to party with on Friday night and another set for Saturday night.

Anyway, once the tummy is clean I eat papaya, followed by cold coffee made with skimmed milk and no sugar. Through the day, I keep my diet light – no carbohydrate, some fruit and a big pot of yoghurt just before stepping out on Saturday night. I love Nestlé skimmed yoghurt. I add a whole lot of roasted cumin and black sesame seeds and salt and it tastes great. It fills the tummy and lines it, and gets it ready for more champagne.

Now, here is the killer or the strawberry in the champagne. Dieticians and trainers still reading, please look away. I have lost weight on this diet. And had some of my greatest nights out. The buzz of champagne does not allow you to feel deprived even though you are not eating. But it's purely short term. Because the weight loss is largely on account of dehydration and minimal food. This diet is not sustainable and will probably kill you in the long run. Hey, you heard it from Ajit at the beginning of this section!

The Champagne Diet*

FRIDAY NIGHT
Dinner: Champagne
No restrictions, as many glasses as you can handle but absolutely nothing else.
Lots of dancing

SATURDAY
Wake up: Kunjal kriya
Workout
Breakfast: Papaya, cold coffee with skimmed milk and without sugar
Lunch: Any cooked vegetable or salad
Tea: Bowl of fruit
Early dinner: Big pot of yoghurt
Dinner: Champagne. *No restrictions, as many glasses as you can handle but absolutely nothing else.*

SUNDAY
Wake up: Kunjal kriya
No workout. Day off.
Breakfast: Papaya, cold coffee
Lunch: Cooked vegetables or salad, tawa-roasted paneer
Tea: Fruit, cold coffee, digestive biscuits
Early dinner: Yoghurt

* You can replace the champagne with sparkling wine if you like. But it doesn't work with any other alcohol.

WEIGHT LOST:
1 kg

WISDOM GAINED:

Here's to breaking every sensible dietary rule and losing weight anyway. Santé!

DIET #39 ● AGE 38 ● WEIGHT 59 KG

ONE WEEK WITH BULIMIA

This is not really a diet but it is one way of losing weight. Let's just say it's an alternative. It's a sickness, really. The medical description is 'bingeing and purging'. Yo-yo dieting is a bit like that and this is an extreme form of it. The net is full of tips on how to do it right. Pro-bulimia sites. We live in a crazy world. Do skip this chapter too if you are queasy. Because it is not pretty. And it is definitely not politically correct.

I decided to experiment with bulimia. I was curious. After all, I did yogic cleansing once a week. The morning purge felt good and removed any fear of purging from my mind. And it was a natural progression – if you can purge on an empty stomach, why not on a full stomach and all the time? How easy to be able to eat everything and then stick your fingers down your throat and bring it all out. It's like having the cake and the icing and then not having it at all. Calorie-free bingeing, the ultimate dieter's fantasy.

This is different from anorexia, where you eat nothing because you believe you are overweight and cannot afford any calories. Bulimics stuff themselves till they are at bursting point and then purge so that they don't consume any calories. Well, that's what it looked like from the other side. I was tempted and convinced myself that it was in the interest of the book that I try it out for a week.

First, I needed to get over the eek factor. It is not easy forcing yourself to vomit. I thought the yogic cleansing would help. But as I discovered with my first purge, it's not really the same thing because with kunjal kriya the cleansing is done first thing in the morning on an empty stomach. The purge is clean. Tasteless, odourless and colourless. Bulimic purging is done on an overfull stomach.

How I did it

I improvised on the technique of kunjal kriya. I drank a couple of glasses of warm water, I found a clean toilet and experimented. (The first few times I did it in the sink but food bits got stuck in the drain and the water got logged and it was disgusting. Truly disgusting.)

I washed my hands and stuck my clean fingers down my throat soon after eating. This worked the first few times. But each session required more than one purge, and to get it all out I had to push my fingers deep down (I had to remember to cut my nails!). Then I learnt that rather than deep diving it was easier to tickle the back of my throat, which had a natural gagging response. I repeated the action till my tummy was empty. It came out quite easily. I drank glasses of water to make the stuff come up easier but found Diet Coke the most helpful. The food came out in the reverse order of how I ate it, so when the first thing I ate came up, I knew it was time to stop. I did this experiment for about a week.

Purging is different from throwing up involuntarily. This food is not rotten or stale so it does not have the sour taste and smell of vomit. It is a bit like tasting the same food again. Double taste, no calories. Gross.

How long after bingeing did I purge?

The first few times I was pretty unsure about the experiment so I would rush off straight after the meal. But by the end of the week I could wait for almost an hour before I rushed off to the bathroom. Maybe the body starts adjusting and delays the digestion process, knowing it's all going to come out anyway. Even an hour after eating I had no problem purging all the food.

How I felt

I did not feel weak or malnourished as I had feared. I went through my bulimia diet without any problem and did all my regular activities, including working out. I felt hungry more quickly, even though I was eating huge meals. And I ate more because I knew I was going to throw it up. I stopped at no number of helpings, I just kept eating till I felt sick because that was the point.

I did not put on any weight but I did not lose weight either. My throat felt sore and my ears, jaws and eye sockets hurt from all the purging. By the end of the week, my throat felt like it was on fire. Purging puts a lot of pressure on the facial muscles. My skin looked sallow, my eyes had sunk in and my face was lined.

Occupational hazards

The retching can be unpredictable and the trajectory of food projectiles is unknown. This can create quite a messy situation. And trust me, you don't want to know more.

My mouth felt dry and my teeth were coated with acid for a long time after the purge. I needed to keep a toothbrush handy.

On a couple of occasions when I had eaten spicy food, the purge was very acidic and it burnt my throat. I kept lozenges with me to make it better.

In the end, it got pretty tiresome. I had to plan where I was eating, when I could get away, make sure there was a loo nearby and no one hovering around. You can't really do this in people's homes – or at least, I didn't have the guts to do so. And public toilets are risky because the sound of retching is a dead giveaway.

Besides, the whole thing took too much time. Every purging session took at least fifteen minutes. And it felt pointless to enjoy a lovely meal and then just flush it away. Such a waste.

The return from the dark side

But I see how it can get addictive. I was getting there. It was no longer an extreme alternative diet. In just over a week, it was almost becoming a habit. I started liking that starved feeling and any food in my stomach made me feel uncomfortable.

But I was saved. On one of my purges, the water from the toilet bowl splashed into my face, blinding my eyes. Even with a clean bowl this is not a hygienic or remotely fun wake-up call. And this experiment was flushed down the toilet once and for all.

WEIGHT LOST: None

WISDOM GAINED: Flush this diet down the toilet. It's not good for weight loss, only for wrinkle gain.

DIET #40 • AGE 38 • WEIGHT 62 KG

YOU CAN, I CAN, LET'S DO THE CANCAN

What's good enough for a princess is good enough for me. The latest star in the royal circle is supposed to have followed this diet to drop many sizes before her wedding. It's the new diet on the fat block. It is apparently the reason why French women are so thin. I picked up the book and decided to give it a shot.

I thought the diet was pretty cool. It was divided into three stages: the pure protein stage, the protein plus vegetable stage, and the stabilizing stage, followed by the diet for life.

Dr CanCan has obviously treated enough patients to paint an accurate picture of the advantages and pitfalls of the diet. He explains what happens at every stage and why. He has several useful weightloss tips. His book is simple to follow as the diets are written day by day and he elaborates on each step. He tells you how much weight you can expect to lose and how long you need to follow each dietary stage. The book also explains that unless the diet is followed through all its stages, the weight comes back on.

And it is honest. It does not sidestep the not-so-pleasant side-effects of the diet, like a dry mouth that tastes a bit like gun metal. On the third day, I felt like even my body was smelling. Small side-effects for big gains.

To tell you the truth, I just liked the drastic weightloss promises. I can't do the one-kilo-a month diets. And this book promised about 3 kg in five days with the first stage. I was hooked.

In the first five days you are allowed ten kinds of food, including meat, fish, non-fat dairy, eggs and oat bran. This is a not a high-protein diet; it is an *only* protein diet. Now I am a fussy non-vegetarian. I like sanitized pieces of meat, no bones, no skin, no shape. A high-protein non-vegetarian diet is not a dream for me. I wanted to ask whether I could include soya or tofu or dal or paneer. You could call the dietician and ask him what else you can eat. Except, he is inside a book. Book dieticians don't answer questions, so it can be rather frustrating. For me, eggs, fat-free flavoured yoghurt and skimmed milk were the staples of this diet.

The diet also emphasizes drinking water. It says the combination of water and protein is magic for breaking down cellulite. I had to have at least a litre-and-a-half of water each day.

The other revelation was one-and-a-half tablespoons of oat bran a day. Oat bran is a great low-cal filler. It expands in the tummy and makes you feel full. I loved it. But maybe my tastebuds had been numbed. When I suggested it to my father as a low-cal, easy to conjure up snack option for the office, he was very excited and got himself a box at once. Later I asked him how it worked for him and he said, 'I tried everything. I put honey, nuts, raisins, banana and I tried hard to gulp it down but I just couldn't. Then I decided life can't be about this and ordered myself some chaat. How could you eat this stuff for so many days?' Well, I can, you can, we all can do the CanCan.

My Version of the Only-protein Diet

Wake up: Tea
Workout
Breakfast: Cold coffee made with half glass skimmed milk, no sugar and lots of ice, 2 egg-white omelet with mustard
Lunch: 2 tbsp oat bran mixed with skimmed milk
Tea: Cold coffee made with half glass skimmed milk, no sugar and lots of ice, 2 egg-white omelet / 4 slices turkey ham with Tabasco
Dinner: 2 pots fat-free yoghurt / grilled fish marinated in mint chutney

After ten days, of this I began the next stage where I was allowed to add vegetables to my protein diet. This was a relief. I was craving carrots and on day one I had them for breakfast. This stage made going out convenient as it was easy to order a protein and vegetable meal. I followed it for five days and then returned to the protein diet for five days. I did this for a total of three weeks. It was tough but the result was so satisfying it kept me going.

WEIGHT LOST:	WISDOM GAINED:
4 kg in 21 days	When a diet is tough it really works

Explosive rebound

Once you have lost the weight you want, you gradually introduce other food groups to your diet. For the rest of your life, you are supposed to follow the only-protein diet once a week.

Most dieters fall off at this stage, as they are so pleased with the results. I meant to follow the phases properly but before I could start on the next stage, I went on a holiday where I bought oat bran on day one but opened a pack of dark chocolate-chip muffins instead.

After a three-week holiday, the weight was back. It came quicker than ever. I was up by 4 kg. That has never happened. The book warns against this: if you don't follow the stages properly, the weight will come back with a vengeance. But who heeds good advice?

While I was on holiday in Europe, it was *the* diet. I quizzed all those I met who were on it and found that most people just did the first phase and lapsed and then went back to it. I did not come across a single person who had done all the stages of the diet as laid out in the book. In that sense, the diet is a victim of its own success. It is so effective you feel you can let go and just get back into shape by doing the protein phase again. I am sure that's not good for you. Everyone I met who followed it lost a lot of weight but they did not necessarily look healthy. They looked somewhat gaunt and wrinkled.

But what a great weapon to fight the battle of the bulge. It may not give you undisputed victory but it holds off the fat for long enough. And when the choice is between looking like a fat frog or a gaunt princess, I will take the princess every time, thank you very much. Back to I can, you can, let's do the CanCan.

WEIGHT GAINED: 5 kg in 3 weeks

WISDOM GAINED: You can win the battle against the bulge with intensive forays but you can't win the war!

DIET #41 • AGE 38 • WEIGHT 60 KG
JAI MATA DI!

I have heard it so many times: 'It's okay, I will go on a navratra fast just before Diwali, nine days of fasting will fix everything. Jai Mata Di!' It was that time of year when I was having some lumpy issues that could do with some divine intervention.

The navratra fast is based on an ancient tradition of fasting for nine days, to detox the body in preparation for the festive season. Before the heavy loading, unloading was required. The rules of the fast have got a bit confused over time. And there are many generalizations and customizations by devotees. These are the principles I understood and decided to follow:

- No cereal. Instead of cereal, fasters use kuttu ka atta to make their puris or rotis. Kuttu ka atta is flour made of buckwheat. It is high in protein and fibre and low on taste. The perfect diet food. I could also eat samak ke chawal, faster's rice. This is the seed of a grass that frequently grows among rice paddy. It looks a lot like soft broken rice. It is high in fibre and quite tasty.

- No salt is allowed except sendha namak or rock salt.
- No alcohol and no non-vegetarian food.
- You are allowed a very restricted list of vegetables such as potato, pumpkin, bottle gourd, arbi and water chestnut, which are prepared without onions, garlic or ginger.
- All fruit, milk and milk products like paneer and yoghurt are allowed in unlimited quantities. God is truly kind.

As potato and milk products are allowed in all kinds of preparations, they are the staple for most fasters. A divine licence to eat French fries and vegetarian ice-cream. Like I said, god is kind and he is definitely not a dietician!

Mostly, fasters restrict themselves to one cooked meal a day, when they eat the specified vegetables cooked under special guidelines with rotis or puris or rice made with the stipulated ingredients. The rest of the day they eat fruit, milk, yoghurt. The fast can be kept for a maximum of nine days and a minimum of one.

I was amazed at the navratra food industry. I discovered special vrat biscuits, saboo dana chidwa, navratra thalis at restaurants and office canteens. Many shops used the restrictive ingredients to churn out yummy dishes like tikkis, puris and pakodas. Some diet this was going to be.

I thought, I have done severe diets, this will be easy. No time or quantity restrictions on fruit, milk, yoghurt. Plus, one cooked meal a day and legit snacks through the day. I decided I would do all nine days.

I was now officially a navratri. The evening of completing the first day of the fast, I told my housekeeper I was keeping the fast for the next eight days and began to explain my food requirements.

She looked sceptical and told me, 'Didi, now you have become very issmart, why are you dieting?'

I told her, unconvincingly, 'I am not dieting.'

'You will just be in a bad mood for no reason and there is no need, you are fit now,' she said.

'Arre, I am not dieting,' I told her irately.

She said, 'Okay, you are not dieting, you are doing the navratra fast. Then did you do the pooja-path before you ate today?'

I was stumped. She had me. Then she said haughtily, 'You better light a diya and pray before you eat tomorrow morning,' and sashayed off. Okay then!

From day two, I prayed every morning before I began my diet and followed it through religiously. It added a whole new dimension to the diet. The fear of god. This was no longer just a diet, it was bigger than that, it was about the strength of my devotion. Breaking the diet could incur the wrath of god. If there ever was a reason to eat only French fries for dinner and stick to a diet, this was it. For blessing and moksha.

They say you fast and take mannat for something and your faith in that one thing is so strong that you don't feel hungry. Mata curbs your hunger. Well, she was not very gentle with me. On day four of the fast, I was reading the newspaper in the morning and saw an insert by Haldiram advertising their navratra thali with paneer makhani and chaat and aloo tikki. I was so hungry I almost ate the leaflet. Strictly speaking, paper is within the rules of the navratra fast and it would have tasted better than kuttu!

There is mention of fasting in many Indian religious scriptures. Fasting helps create an attunement with the absolute by establishing a harmonious relationship between the body and the soul. You are expected to live piously, to give charity and to refrain from eating non-vegetarian food while fasting. Okay, BIG fail on that count. I was super cranky and was not eating toast but two children, one husband and all other sundry for breakfast!

According to Ayurveda, the body is composed of 80 per cent liquid and 20 per cent solid, and, like the earth, the gravitational force of the moon affects the fluid content of the body. It causes emotional imbalances in the body, making some people tense, irritable or violent. Fasting acts as an antidote, as it lowers the acid content in the body, which helps people retain their sanity. By day five, I thought I might need to break the fast if I wanted to maintain mine. The image of the thali and the chaat would not leave my mind. And I was anything but calm.

But fasting is a great way to inculcate self-discipline and to test your will power. It was tough but I survived. Jai Mata Di!

The JMD Diet

Early morning: Tea, cardio workout for one hour
Breakfast: Tea, a bowl of papaya/pomegranate/1 pear
Mid-morning: Skimmed milk cappuccino
Lunch: Kuttu roti (though it was more like a paratha), mashed pumpkin sabzi cooked with the skin, with no onion, no garlic / Samak rice, paneer in a tomato gravy with no onion, no garlic / Samak rice, arbi in a tomato gravy with no onion, no garlic and aloo and saboo dana ki tikki, low-fat yoghurt
Tea: Cappuccino and navratra saboo dana chidwa / Kuttu navratra biscuits / 2 dried apricots
Dinner: Tea with mirchi aloo chips / Sliced banana with low-fat yoghurt, almonds, black and green raisins and honey / 2 glasses of cold coffee without ice-cream

WEIGHT LOST:
2 kg in 9 days

WISDOM GAINED:
God is not a dietician.

DIET #42 ● AGE 38 ● WEIGHT 62 KG

RUNNING TO STAY ON THE SAME SPOT

Maintenance is a many-lettered word but it behaves like a four-letter word. Compared to maintaining it, losing weight is much easier. It's hard to stay on track if what you arc doing is a program and not a way of life. If you have been following a stuffing-and-lazing routine for most of your life, changing track permanently is not easy.

I have lost the same weight many times. You can be a victim of your own success. The more successful you are at losing weight and doing it quickly, the more relaxed you are about putting it back on. You know you can always lose it again. For this reason, it's important to remember how far you have come, to remind yourself constantly how hard it really is and how easy to slip back.

Maintaining the weight is the hardest part of the equation. Once you have reached your target weight, the motivation is gone. And all the help is gone. You are on your own and this can be quite intimidating at first but you have to stick in there. My dietician gave me the first push, saying she was not going to give me a diet any more. She said I now knew enough to do the right thing by my body.

In case of emergency break this glass

Here is what happened to me in spite of all that I know. An overindulgent holiday continued well after I came back home. Not because of lack of intent. I wanted to get back on track but was finding it impossible. The constant fighting between craving and good sense carried on for a whole week after the holiday. Craving kept winning the battle. I was losing the plot and the diet but not the weight.

To top it all, I had a dizzy spell a few times and the doctor said I had low blood pressure. Everyone started telling me to eat, they all said I had done very well but should quit now. I resisted for a while and then fell right off the wagon. I indulged at every meal, except perhaps breakfast. Rice at lunch. Rice at dinner. Chocolate in all the betweens. Butter biscuits from Chandigarh. Midnight snack of chutney sandwich layered with butter, chutney and bhujiya. Picnics with copious amounts of champagne, egg mayo sandwiches where the egg was incidental, gooey brownies. Late night Nanaimo bars. Nothing was off limit. For a while it was liberating and then it felt terrible. I felt lazy, fat and lacking in energy. I was not particularly enthused about my workouts but somehow managed to do them regularly.

I was not happy. I was not bubbling with energy. All the bulges seemed to be popping out. I had slipped badly. I had to get back on track, and this is the diet I followed to terminate the dark side.

Terminator Diet

I forced myself to do one complete day of the diet properly and made my mind and body accept it. I dedicated my Monday just to getting back on track. It was my top priority of the day. I did not let stress, work or any other obligations come in the way. The single focus of the day was to get back on the diet. It was a very hard day. But it worked. Like Arnold Schwarzenegger famously said, 'I'll be back.'

DAY ONE
8:00 a.m. Masala tea
10:00 a.m. Papaya with lemon
10.50 a.m. Long vent to girlfriend, hungry and emotional about denying myself food.
11.30 a.m. Two cups coffee
1.45 p.m. Salted lassi, bowl of yoghurt with black sesame, cumin and salt

2.30 p.m. Keep myself busy by filling in long-pending baby book and clearing photos. Find old scary photos of self. Now really motivated.

4.30 p.m. Workout

6.00 p.m. Big crying fit about weight being up to 62 kg. Reasoning that it is evening weight doesn't help.

6.30 p.m. Papaya with lemon, cold coffee without sugar. Want to eat one digestive biscuit. NO.

7.45 p.m. Bowl of yoghurt with black sesame, cumin and salt. Want to add a spoon of rajma to the dahi. NO.

8.00 p.m. Shopping

11.00 p.m. Bed

1.30 a.m. Wake up. Can't sleep. Tummy empty. Hunger pangs and nervous energy. Mouth feeling like gun metal. Get out of bed and start writing. Want to keep the experience of getting back on track fresh. Like the energy, don't like the hunger pangs.

DAY TWO

8:00 a.m. Masala tea

9.30 a.m. Workout

10.50 a.m. Weigh in. Yes! Back to 59 kg.

11.00 a.m. Papaya with lemon

11.30 a.m. Meetings

1.45 p.m. Two pots of probiotic yoghurt with salt

2.20 p.m. More meetings

4.30 p.m. Cappuccino

5.00 p.m. Papaya with lemon

6.30 p.m. Salted lassi

8.00 p.m. Masala tea

10.30 p.m. Mind buzzing. Full of energy. But hunger pangs and dreaming of food. Just have to stick to it. Hunger pangs good. Means diet is effective.

Day Three is the hardest. But the weight is off and that's motivation. To keep it off and to make it permanent, I have to stick to the diet one more day. And I do.

WEIGHT LOST:

2 kg

WISDOM GAINED:

Good habits are great but bad habits are so much easier.

WORKOUT #43 ● AGE 38 ● WEIGHT 61.8 KG

AMERICAN ENTERTRAINER

My timing changed as the kids' school timings changed and I needed another trainer. I discovered the American Gangsta Rapsta Playa. Goatee, beanie, low trackpants revealing red boxers, tattoos on his arms, trendy sneakers and the trademark swagger. He was unusual for a trainer in Delhi. He was half American and half Indian and chose his nationality according to his convenience and audience. He was a trainer by day and a DJ by night. When he said hi, his body language said, 'Yo girl 'ssup.'

He was a certified MMA (mixed martial artist) fighter. When I first met him, he was training for a free-for-all knockout fight night, which he eventually won, almost killing his opponent. There was no messing around with him. I would have been terrified, but for one thing.

His regularity was a bit like Russian roulette. I was to train with him thrice a week but never knew in the morning whether he would turn up. Very often I would get a message at six a.m., citing some excuse or the other – sick, car puncture, car locked in by the neighbours, blah blah blah. Trained MMA or not, I was ready to kill him just with dirty looks, and if that did not work, with my bare hands. I had become religious about my workout and his attitude bugged me. In the end, I had to give him the 'what are you doing with your life and career' lecture. He was just lax, a little too fond of partying and of his other life as a DJ. After the lecture, he gave up DJing on the nights before he was training me. Respect.

When he did come, we got on well. Warmups were like catching up with a girlfriend. Great for me, a little worrying for him. My workouts with him were cardio-centred. He said if I wanted to lose fat I had to do more cardio and less weights. Cardio melts fat. Strength or weight training tightens specific muscles. Fat loss cannot be targeted. Whatever, I needed cardio. We had moved to a new house away from the Rose Garden. Now I lived around a small colony garden, big enough to train in. It became my torture chamber and morning entertainment for all the drivers and gardeners.

I started running around the colony, against a stopwatch, with Entertrainer standing at the end of the lane to stop the traffic so I would not have to break my step. Like I was some athlete training for a marathon. Respect.

He took me to the next level. I had been running regularly but to crank it up a notch, I had to do fitness moves from basketball, cricket and boxing. And there was circuit training with jumping jacks, plank pushups, burpies (which are similar to squat thrusts), mountain climbing. And I had to skip. I had never skipped as a child. Duh! That must be obvious. Now I had to skip in a fancy hip hop style. It was a disaster. First, the rope was not right. Then the length was not right. Then the mat was not right.

Plank Pushup

Then my ponytail was not right. When I finally got all of that right, I managed to skip. Once. The Entertrainer was disgusted but to his credit, he continued to train with me. He broke it down to hand and leg movements and helped me with the coordination. After much trial and error, I finally got it. Ungraceful and stumbling, I managed to do thirty continuously. 'Yeaaaah baby, thas wut ahm talkin bout, you gettin pretty good with the rope yo.' Respect.

The workout gave me more definition and better fitness but made me thinner only in the weeks that I supplemented it with a diet. Without a strict diet, that's the best even a tough workout can do.

> *Hip hop and skip, if ya wanna lose those hips*
> *But to make ya weight dip ya gotta seal those lips*
> *So lace ya Nikes and zip up ya mouth*
> *The Entertrainer's here n it's time to work out!*

WEIGHT LOST:
A couple of kilos yo-yoing

WISDOM GAINED:
A playa can only supply you with the stuff, he can't make you take it!

THE ROUTE NOT TO TAKE

SHORTCUT TO SKINNY

Why sweat and toil when there are easier ways to lose weight?

Why not just go for a lunch-break surgery and come back thin? Many people have said to me, 'You must have had surgery, this kind of weight loss can't be for real.' Well, it is. I did think about surgery but always shied away, even though surgery is becoming the answer to every problem in a society fixated with looking perfect. Botox, pumped lips, breast enhancements, lipo. And it is getting increasingly safer and easier to do. It's an alternative lunch date. You go in the morning and are back home in the afternoon. There are not even six degrees of separation between people who have had it and those who haven't. You probably know somebody yourself who has had a procedure. But I didn't opt for surgery and there are many reasons for it.

Honey, I went for lunch and shrunk my hips!

At 5'3" and 104 kg I was the ideal candidate. I was medically obese and had enough fat to justify surgery. It was not just for cosmetic reasons. My fat was a danger to my health and surgery could be medically prescribed – a weightloss surgery like stomach stapling or a gastric bypass where they would shrink the size of my tummy through surgery, or even something less drastic and more cosmetic like liposuction or a tummy tuck would have given me instant results.

I didn't opt for the shortcut. There is a certain pride in looking the way you do because you worked for it. I saw surgery as invasive Photoshop. There is no joy in looking great with unnatural enhancements.

I also believe that the harder you work to look a certain way, the more committed you are to keeping it that way. If you lose weight the easy way, the incentive to keep it off is not there. You did not put blood and sweat into it and are not going to remember how hard it is to keep it off. You went under general anesthesia and you came out thin. Voila!

Liquify

I work in the media business and my works involves looking at many fashion and women's magazines. I see the raw images of stars and the touched-up images. It pains me to see the pressure the media creates for real women who feel the need to look like the unreal ones on our magazine covers. But it is now such a vicious cycle that the stars expect it, the advertiser expects it and the reader expects it. Everyone expects you to smooth out the bumps and lumps. And the processes and tools have become so sophisticated. The photographer shoots digitally and alters the image right there at the shoot. The latest softwares have a tool called liquify. It's a magic wand that can just contour the body to a perfect ten in seconds, which would be hard to achieve over years of dieting and workouts. Celebrities, whose full-time job is to look good, need Photoshop and expect the liquify tool. And if they can't manage a perfect ten or even an eight, what chance do real women have? So give yourself a break. Those cheekbones, those curves, that jaw line have been created in most cases by a designer on a laptop.

Slim thighs and thunder lips

Liposuction gives you instant results but to maintain it you have to stick to a proper diet and exercise programme. Otherwise it comes back. With a tummy tuck, it is worse. If you put on weight and the skin can't expand, it's like wearing a tight-suit all the time. And since the body can't expand in the areas that have had surgery, it starts expanding abnormally in other parts. So the tummy will remain flat but the fat comes back on your thighs or bottom. This is a medical fact. A new study has revealed that the fat removed by liposuction returns and gets 'redistributed upstairs' – around the shoulders, arms and upper abdomen – after a year. Rudolph Leibel, an obesity researcher at the University of Columbia, told the *New York Times* that the body controls the number of fat cells as carefully as it controls the amount of fat. When a fat cell dies, it grows a new one to replace it. Liposuction, however, surgically destroys the fishnet structure under the skin, which may be why fat cells don't re-grow in the place from which they were removed. Instead, the body compensates for the loss by growing new fat cells in other areas. Liposuction fat is back within a year. What's taken from the thighs returns on the arms. If only it returned on the lips, it might have been some consolation!

The first cut is the deepest

The first surgery is the hardest. Once you take the leap there is no looking back. Most people who have one procedure end up going back for another. It's addictive.

Surgery is an irreversible change; you have to keep going back for maintenance. The surgery route requires regular touch ups. But unlike a healthier lifestyle change that includes changes in diet and exercise, surgery is governed by a law of diminishing returns. Over time, the more you do the less effective it is, whereas with dietary control and exercise there is a multiplier effect.

While surgery may be the magic wand every fat person fantasizes about, it only gets you there faster; to stay thin you need to change your lifestyle. Those who have their tummy shrunk have to eat smaller portions for life. Inability to do so leads to immediate nausea and if you persist with overeating, the stomach expands to its original size over time and the benefits of the surgery are lost. Research on weightloss surgery patients shows that though excess weight is lost initially, a large number of people regain the lost weight after 3 to 5 years if they don't change their lifestyle.

Flat abs or flat line

Surgery can go wrong. People die on the surgery table. I could not risk my life for a smaller bum. The trade-off did not work for me. And I am too squeamish. I can barely stand reading about cuts, tubes being forced in, drainage of liquids and sutures, let alone face the actual procedure.

The reading material says it's not a pain that can't be dealt with with a normal painkiller. Read this excerpt. Do you buy their claim?

Post-operative Healing

Pain after tumescent liposuction of the abdomen typically does not require any pain medications stronger than acetaminophen (Tylenol). The quality of the pain is similar to the muscle soreness and burning experienced after having worked-out too much. The intensity of the pain is similar to that of a sunburn; it is most intense when the skin of the area is flexed or touched, such as getting in and out of a car, or rolling-over in bed, or when sitting still in a chair. There is minimal discomfort when walking or sitting.
OUCH!

Swelling and Soreness

The day after surgery, as a result of open-drainage (incisions are not closed with sutures) of the blood-tinged anesthetic fluid and wearing a compression garment, the degree of cosmetic improvement is easily visible and quite dramatic. Over the next several days, after the drainage has ceased, and as the inflammatory healing process progresses, there is a gradual onset of swelling which decreases over the following 4 to 12 weeks. A certain degree of swelling, firmness and lumpiness is normal for the first 4 to 12 weeks. This firmness of the abdominal skin and subcutaneous tissue gradually decrease over 3 to 4 months after surgery.

Courtesy www.liposuction.com

Tummytuck vs Liposuction

Liposuction sucks the fat out from under the skin; a tummy tuck will reduce the fat and tighten the loose skin.

Liposuction is advisable if you have minimal weight to lose on your abdomen – less than 15 kg – and don't have loose skin. A tummy tuck is better if you have looseness in that area.

From a medical point of view, liposuction is a relatively simple procedure. A thin, hollow tube is inserted into the body and the fat is sucked out. There is minimal scarring and the recovery time is quick. A tummy tuck is a far more complex procedure. A huge cut is made just above the pubic area and abdominal muscles and the skin is pulled tight and sewn back up. There is more scarring and higher chances of things going wrong.

Finally, liposuction is far cheaper than a tummy tuck.

A spanxing good contraption

Spanx. The ultimate corset underwear to iron out all the inconvenient bits. No surgery required. It just puts everything in place, in one neat package. It's made of soft, cling-free yarn and comes in many versions. When you go to their website you feel like a fat person in a candy store. There are different types depending on the kind of dress you want to wear and the bits of fat you want to smooth out – tummy taming, thigh trimming, butt boosting. It comes in many shapes – panty, body suit, shape suit, skinny britches, open bust, mid thigh, body suit, super-high footless shaper, etc. And in varying degrees of slimming strength – medium, super, super duper.

The woman who set it up is a millionaire and a genius. Her line now includes swimwear and even Spanx for men.

I am not a big fan of this. First, because it feels like cheating. Second, you can tell it from a mile away. It's fine for the red carpet and all the stars swear by it, but the minute somebody gives you a hug they know something is not quite right. Besides, it stops circulation to such a large extent that you have no sensation. Once, a friend of mine had her whole bum felt up by an acquaintance and she didn't even feel it. Her Spanx were in place. Third, it is a real ceremony to put on and mine never stayed in place. They were always rolling down or cutting into some soft squishy bit of me or pushing something in and making it stick out somewhere else. I would rather do an extra set of pushups than get into that contraption. Fourth, if you were worried about undressing in front of your lover in your comfortable granny underpants, banish all thoughts of sexy undressing when wearing one of these great-grandmothers!

But hey, they are getting better every season and, who knows, they might have the perfect one for me too. And who doesn't need a slimming hand once in a while?

WISDOM GAINED:

There are no shortcuts to heaven. If you want a bit of help to get into that dress, get the Spanx, not the surgery.

8

THE SECRETS

You already have a kilo-by-kilo account of how
I got from 100 to 60. Here are the secrets that
have travelled through many diets and workouts
to reach you.

MOTIVATORS

I only lost weight when I decided to. No one else could make that decision for me. The calling came from inside. I have been on many diets and yo-yo'd serially. I spent a long time trying to find the trigger that motivates me and gets me back on track each time. I thought, if I could find the trigger that starts it all and share it with others, it would be supremely helpful. Every time a fat person goes off track, all you have to do is pull the right trigger to get them back. And I have found the trigger.

Love.

Nothing gets the fat (or, for that matter, the world) moving like love. It's the super motivator, the magic pill that every fat person fantasizes about. It can be love of any kind. For a lover, for children, for an object of desire, for yourself (this last is the hardest but the most important). Wanting to look good for someone or to be able to do something for someone is a super motivator.

When I was in my tweens, I was motivated by my love for horses. I was obsessed with horses and spent all my time at the stables. I first lost weight because I wanted a new saddle. It was the carrot that was dangled in front of me.

At my skinniest, I was motivated by my then-lover-now-husband. I wanted to surprise him with my new look. I wanted to look my best for him so that we could do all the things we wanted to, together. And I did. I surprised him so much that he asked me to marry him.

And now? My family and friends always ask me, why now? Well, what finally clicked for me after twelve years of marriage were my children. When I was fat I couldn't keep up with them. I was lethargic, lazy and cranky. I wanted to set a good example for them. They could only be healthy if they saw it around them.

I did not want to be a burden on them in my old age and if I continued on the fat path I was going to be old before my time and riddled with problems. To give them my very best, I needed to be healthy. And I could not be the best mother I could be at 100 kg.

Of course, once the weight started coming off, many things started changing and I was now doing it for the other positives it brought to my life.

If you are not in love, fall in love. Immediately.

TRICKS TO GETTING THIN AND STAYING THERE

The supportive husband

My husband is definitely my better half! He has always been extremely supportive. It's difficult to walk this path on your own. You need a support system that encourages you and puts up with the temper tantrums caused by denial. My husband is Mr Fix-it. He always had the perfect solution to my tantrums. He was soothing and supportive. I was never pressured to join him for dinner at the table, for a night out or an evening drink.

Often, he would sit at home with me if my diet was too restrictive to allow going out. Or he would eat dinner alone at the dining table. He was happy to have a healthy kitchen rather than insist on desserts and goodies. It's important to include your husband or significant other in your weightloss plan.

The perfect dress

Picture yourself in your fantasy outfit, whether it's a Bond bikini or a Cinderella gown.

Mine was the dress for the France wedding. All I thought about was that dress. When I tried it on the first time, I knew I wanted it tighter, sharper, sexier. My back had to look good. I could not have a paunch. I had to have toned arms. Every time I thought I couldn't do it any more, I just thought of the dress. The dress was larger than life.

Your best accessory

A great body is your best accessory. Nothing makes a hotter statement than a toned body. When I realized it is not clothes that make a woman but the body, things began to fall in place. Not even the custom-ordered fuchsia pink Herve Leger bandage-dress can make up for that tyre. The Bottega wedges can't take away from the thunder thighs. The Chanel lipstick doesn't hide the double chin. But a pair of non-branded jeans with a white shirt and hawai chappals on a fit body can make heads turn.

Throw away your fat clothes

Keep the wardrobe fat-free. Don't hoard oversize clothes. Throw away the fat clothes. Trust yourself never to become that weight again. Having larger clothes you can fit into as you put on a few kilos is a deterrent to weight loss. It makes you comfortable. Alter them or get rid of them. Have fewer things but things that fit. It will keep you on track. A lean wardrobe, a lean you.

Tell everyone

Don't be shy about your efforts to lose weight. Instead, get all your friends and family to invest in your weight loss. The more people you tell, the more people will look at you questioningly when you eat that dessert or order that pizza. They'll say, 'What happened to your diet?' Or they will pass a snide remark like, 'Oh, having a day off?' This is irritating but supremely useful. I have even taught my kids to be my watchdogs on holiday. When they see me eating chocolate or a muffin, they pipe up, 'Mama, what about your diet?'

You have to eat right because you have to live up to your own reputation and rules.

Party party party

Going out when you are losing weight is essential. Dressing up and looking good is an important part of the routine. It is therapy for your tired muscles, a soothing balm for your willpower. The compliments keep you going. Show your stuff. Flaunt it. Enjoy people telling you 'I can hardly recognize you!', 'You look stunning!', 'Wow, how did you lose so much weight?' Validation on how far you have come is critical to keep the process going. But be warned: too much of this can go to your head and hamper the weightloss process.

Weigh yourself daily

Decide your average weight. It can vary by 2 kg either side, depending on your menstrual cycle and the time of day. Write down your weight on a piece of paper and paste it where you can see it. If the weight is even 100 gm over the 2 kg allowance, sound the red alert. This is my mother's trick for maintaining her weight. In fact, I don't know why weighing scales don't come with a built-in alert system these days. Once the weight is 3 kg over, it is a sliding road. Under 3 kg can be tackled with a few days' detox and cutting down on food like sweets or carbs for one week. More than that and you need to get onto a programme or you are back on the vicious cycle.

The Dog Is Not Your Best Friend

The weighing scale is your best friend. Talk to it every day. It tells it like it is. It has no agenda. It keeps you on your toes. Never ignore or fight with your best friend. Meet it every day.

Banish some foods for ever

Programme yourself to believe they are poison. French fries. Smileys. Jalebis. Pizza. I have decided I cannot touch these things. Maybe once a year, and even that is more than enough.

Indulge only when something is really worth the calories

Don't eat mindlessly. If melted dark chocolate has been poured over nuts and rolled into a bar in front of you, heck, indulge. But do you really need another one of those cocktail prawns dunked in thick chilli-garlic sauce? NO. And do you have to eat that Smiley off your child's birthday party plate? NO. And is that lemon soufflé in the buffet actually worth the calories? NO. And do you need to eat the rasmalai on the food tray on the flight? NO. Choose what you cheat on. See the section on Golden Calories, calories that are worth their weight in gold.

WHEN THE GOING GETS FAT, THE FAT GO HUNGRY

I am not sure about the tough but the skinny definitely go hungry. It's not easy and there is no magic pill. You just have to shrink the tummy. And shrinkage is not painless. Be under no illusions, you have to walk this road. Most dieticians say, 'My diet will never starve you; there is so much to eat, you will be eating all day.' Yeah, right. They have to say that to convince you to start the journey. Anyone who tells you 'I feel so full on my diet' has done an excellent job of brainwashing themselves. Full marks to them but the truth is, diets are hard in the first stage when the weight loss is just starting. You are going to feel hungry.

In fact, for me a diet is only working if I am hungry, at least in stage one. Or it's like saying you will exercise and lose weight but it won't be strenuous. Of course it will. You have to build your stamina and endurance and soon you will achieve what you want. You will go through hunger pangs. But it will pass. Besides, doing it the hard way will serve as a strong reminder the next time you decide to go on a binge.

Here are a few tricks that helped and still help me deal with the hunger. This is what I do and you can too:

Dinner is not served

I did not enter the dining room. There was no pretence of 'Let's sit at the dinner table and catch up on the day and I will just watch you eat.' Even if you manage to get through dinner without taking a bite, you have sat through a whole meal denying yourself. This denial will be displaced to a craving for other food later. The act of sitting down to dinner gets the mind and body ready to eat food. Why confuse the body with signals that it is getting food when it isn't?

Destock

Destock the kitchen. Nobody needs Oreo cookies, chocolate-chip ice-cream, packets of chips, extra-creamy mature cheddar.

The 'I have a family and children and guests keep coming so I need to keep the fridge stocked' excuse is rubbish. Nobody needs fatty, processed foods. The sooner we teach our kids this, the better.

Whenever a food gift comes to the house, I send it away to friends or tell the staff to finish it immediately. Individually wrapped chocolate brownies announcing a new baby, homemade pista mithai with real silver warq decorations for a wedding shagun, giant bars of Lindt with hazelnut for Diwali … I give them all away instantly. I keep nothing even for a day.

The bottom line is, avoid temptation. If there is chocolate in the house I will eat it, and there was always chocolate in our house before. Now we have chocolate in the house but it is under lock and key and under the supervision of my husband and only for genuine emergencies. He does not relent easily, no matter how angry or how desperate I get for my chocolate fix. I have to be literally dying and on my last breath before he agrees to ration out one piece.

So even when I have a weak moment – and I have many – there is nothing to raid in the kitchen. What am I going to cheat with? The most exciting things in my kitchen are cheese slices and digestive biscuits. Nice, but not quite worth cheating for.

Brainwash yourself

A certain amount of reprogramming is necessary. Your body and mind have been programmed in a certain way and that needs to change. You have to reprogramme your mind. This has to be done on a regular basis as the new programme is prone to viruses. You have to spend time and install regular updates. I have to constantly programme myself into saying:

A holiday does not equal binge eating.
Food does not equal happiness.
Stress does not equal a bar of chocolate.
Weighing myself is like brushing my teeth.

This is some of the new programming that is now hardwired into my system. Repeat after me and every day before you go to sleep and first thing in the morning:

I won't eat when I stress out. I will sweat it out.
I won't eat late at any rate.

I won't skip my workout even if I have to skip work.
I won't forget that dancing, champagne and designer
clothes can feel as good as chocolate.

Disengage from food

For foodaholics, it is essential to wipe out the amount of time and space food occupies in your life. Food has to be displaced from its position of pride within your mind. If, like me, all good things in your life revolve around food and everything is planned around what you are going to eat, change it now.

Food has to be the last thing you plan. I delegate it. I am not in the kitchen cooking it or in the supermarket buying it. I am just not involved. I disengage from meal planning and answering the eternal question that plagues most of us who run a home: 'Aaj dinner ke liye kya banana hai?' What should I make for dinner? I know I'm lucky I have a cook but why does the dinner question always come when I have barely finished lunch? I have made two-week meal plans for my family and left it at that. It has its flaws but overall, the system works.

Do this with your diet plan too. Many diets and dieticians give you recipes and elaborate meal plans to make the diet food you are eating inclusive. I don't believe in that. I think food has to be excluded from your mind space. It's the 'alcoholics can't stop at one drink' approach. You have to stop thinking about food completely.

Reality bites and it's not tasty

I don't believe in making a king's feast out of a meagre diet meal. Diet food is not tasty, get over it. This is my way of dealing with diet food: Just don't think about it. Put it in your mouth to fill your tummy, and move on. No need to savour it and make a ceremony out of it.

Many dieticians say, don't do other things while eating the meal. Let the body fully focus on the fact that it is eating so it knows it is full. Pah! Doesn't work. Just look at the watch, get the right meal out and eat it. Think about this: boardrooms never have windows. You sit in there working for hours without knowing how much time has lapsed or what time of day it is. Your body keeps functioning. Eating follows the same principle. Disengage your mind from the bodily function of hunger.

Lots of diets give you flexibility. This does not work for me. Have a tight plan with contingencies built in. Not too many ifs and buts. Don't give yourself the option of calling your dietician on speed dial. You have a set of rules and you just stick to them. Flexibility is the loophole that allows you to go off the programme because it means thinking about options and engaging with food.

A lot of diets give you tasty fat-free recipes but let's face the facts. Fat is yummy. It's what gives the taste to food. Either you reprogramme what you find tasty or you live with the fact that diet food can never be as satisfying. What I did to make myself feel better was wait to hit a weight milestone and then take a break. Be a little lenient, get comfortable at the new lower weight and then start strict dieting again. You don't have to achieve your ideal target weight in one long endless diet. Give yourself a reasonable timeframe and reward every weight milestone but get back on track.

Green tea

Lots and lots of green tea after six p.m. Most days I just don't enter the front half of my house. I go nowhere in the vicinity of food. Vow not to see your dining table for a while. Retire to your room with a big thermos of green tea and keep sipping it. The tummy might growl but you must labour on.

Green tea is good on many levels. It fills the tummy. It is an excellent antioxidant. And it's a great way to make up your water allowance for the day. And with the lack of food, who says the brain can't imagine green tea with a hint of lemon to taste like lemon cheesecake spiked with green tea ice-cream and three berries tea to taste like fresh fruit sorbet and vanilla chamomile tea to taste like crème brulee?

TV dinners

In the evening, I distract myself with other things that give me pleasure, like watching soap operas or, more recently, writing diet books. Get your support team (in my case, my husband) to record your favourite serials. Come evening and the hunger pangs, switch on the telly and distract your mind. I've watched every season of *Grey's Anatomy*, *Lost*, *Gossip Girl* and *Ugly Betty*, no cupcakes included. I used to be obsessed with downloading the latest episodes. It became my dinner. These days my TV dinner is *The X Factor*.

A growling tummy

When I first started doing it, the no-dinner rule often gave me a headache. I would last till nine p.m. and then my head would start throbbing, largely out of hunger. At this point I had a nice glass of masala tea, rich in elaichi and adrak and with a spoon of Splenda. Dhaba style. On most days this worked quite well and I was able to sleep. On other days I spiked it with a Crocin. The headache would go but I would still lie awake all night on an empty stomach. It took a few weeks to settle down. Now it's the opposite. I can't sleep on a full stomach. It makes me feel uncomfortable.

In case of an emergency, when the tummy just won't stop growling, some fruit or a few spoons of yoghurt or half a glass of skimmed milk will help. This is especially handy if you are having a late night and haven't eaten anything since six.

Trick or treat?

Tick trick every time, here is how:

- ✓ Do something you can tick off on the to-do list. It feels good to keep busy and satisfy the body and mind with fulfilling activities like cleaning or running a pending errand. The feeling of satisfaction on completion is a good substitute for satisfaction from food.
- ✓ Seek therapy other than food. It's important to keep busy with some sort of therapeutic activity between the meagre dinner and bedtime. It keeps the mind occupied.
- ✓ Focusing and reminding yourself of the ugly old days with old photos really helps put the spotlight back on the right track. I never ever want to look like that again.
- ✓ Cry but don't break the diet. Denial of food can make you emotional and cranky and weepy but it's part of the process of letting go. Let the emotion out.
- ✓ Go without sleep but don't succumb. The stomach expands fast. Two weeks of all-you-can-eat and the tummy can't go to sleep without dinner. Remember, the longer you give in, the harder it is to get back.
- ✓ Distract yourself. I survive the diet all day but by evening all I really want is one biscuit, just one digestive biscuit. How much harm can one biscuit do? Enough. Distract, distract, distract. Watch TV, play with your kids, talk to someone.

TRAINING THE TRAINER

I have had many trainers and over the years I have refined the art of getting the best out of them. Personal trainers work. But you need to follow some basic guidelines to ensure that you are getting maximum benefit out of this person.

Go away, I am not getting up today

Don't get a trainer you can shoo away. That does not work. You cannot have a trainer who can be sent home because memsahib is sleeping. If you can sleep through your trainer's visit, change the trainer. He has failed in his primary objective, which is to get you out of bed and into the gym. This is the most important task of the trainer: to ensure you stay committed. You need someone who is tough and who you can't ignore. If he shows up, you show up, or he dumps you. The power balance must be in his favour.

Financial pinch

The fees you pay the trainer should pinch because this gives you added motivation not to bunk your class. You have to sacrifice buying that one extra pair of shoes or lunch or whatever. Don't get the cheap-fix yoga guy for ₹500 who you can work out with endlessly without results. It's a waste of money.

Put the trainer on targets

Be firm. Get a notebook. Write down your measurements. Inches. Kilos. The works. Monitor these monthly. Then the trainer knows he doesn't just have to show up and ensure you get on with it, he has to focus on what you are doing and make sure it is effective. I would tell Hotshot I want to lose 2 kg at the end of the week, I want a 29-inch waist before a party. Unreasonable? Maybe, but it keeps the focus. Once I asked him for shoulder blades like razors, at which point his calm exterior finally cracked and he snapped back, 'I am not a kasai, I am a yoga guru.' Okay, so maybe I pushed it too far.

Like your trainer

I think this is crucial. Like your trainer. You are going to be spending an hour with this individual daily so make sure it's somebody you like. He can't be somebody who irritates you or smells. One of my dear and extremely fit single friends says he sometimes thinks he is not single but married. Married to his trainer. They have been training together for ten years.

Your trainer becomes your sounding board. My latest cardio trainer tells me that he has to be a psychotherapist half the time to his clients because they tell him all the stuff that is on their mind. This makes sense. You are at your most vulnerable, you have told this person your darkest fears, all the things you hate about your body. He has seen you in a naked light.

You need to be able to trust your trainer. You need to make a connection, a bond. If you find somebody who knows your body, stick to him or her. Wait it out but find the right trainer. After all, you have to wake up to this person every morning.

But don't get overfriendly or overfamiliar. There is a thin line. Maintain it.

Give them authority

Never undermine your trainer's authority. This is self-defeating. If you don't give him the authority to push you, to scream at you, to torture you, it won't work. He has to keep you on track. Respect his position. Allow him to have the final word in the gym. No stomping off.

In the end it's not the trainer, it's you

In the end, don't get overdependent on one trainer. At one point, when I lost significant weight with one trainer, I was frantic about putting it back on. It made me unreasonably anxious. I thought, if I stopped training with him I would become fat and my old life would come back. I found that many of my friends who had personal trainers had the same issue. They thought if they pulled the plug they would balloon again.

The editor of *Men's Health* magazine, who had watched my progress with interest, told me, 'You know, your weight loss and achievement are your own. Your trainer helped you but he is not the key. You are. Don't get too dependent.' I think he had seen enough dieters and people proud of their new bodies to see my obvious anxiety. I took his advice. I slowly weaned away from my dependence and flew solo, and it worked. It was good advice that came at a good time.

I still work out with a personal trainer now because I think it adds more discipline to the workout. But I am not dependent on one trainer. I know I can walk this road myself.

GONE WITH THE WEIGHT

Same wine in a different bottle is not the same wine. You can be the same person but in a new body and the world around you changes.

The eternal dilemma

I have realized that my weight is the centrepiece of my life. It is the guiding light and force. Other things have remained constant – love, money, job. But my weight has fluctuated and determined everything in my state of being. This is sad because it ultimately means that my appetite has determined my whole life.

Once I bumped into Anil Ambani at a conference and we got talking. He told me how he was overweight till he made the switch in his head. He said to me, 'You need to decide whether you live to eat or eat to live.' At the time, I thought this was just a clever phrase but the dilemma came back to me years later and now I know those words are rooted in deep wisdom.

You are what you eat because food and how you feel about your body determine your attitude, your state of being towards everything else. People around me say I am happier as a person, apparently more giving and loving than I used to be. I can feel the change too, I am not as cranky and irritable as I used to be. It is no coincidence that I am also healthier and happier with my weight.

Self-doubt

I am not sure how I look. My self-image is confused. Those who love me said I looked wow at 79 kg. How do I trust them when they say the same thing at 59 kg? Is looking stunning relative or absolute? I am obsessed with this question. Am I absolutely thin or just thin compared to what I used to be? I am always wondering.

At over 100 kg I had no problem going out, but at 59 kg I have issues. Once you start focusing on your body you see it in such harsh light that it is impossible to pass any test. Every bulge is an eyesore. I don't want any of it. I want it perfect. Tight, flat, toned, curved, skinny.

Real curves ahead

I am a beach bum but I am never going to have a bikini body. Stretch marks, loose skin, cellulite. My husband says, 'It's hardly the most important thing in the world. So what if you don't look beach-perfect?' First of all, husband, you failed the reassurance test. You are supposed to say I look great. Second, it is important. I love beach holidays. Not being able to look good at doing what I love is not great. Alas, the abuse I have inflicted on my body over the years cannot be wiped clean entirely.

I told the editor of *Good Housekeeping* magazine, who was chasing me for my weightloss story, that my legs were not beach-ready yet and she said to me, 'What are two legs when you have two arms, a face, a neck, a stomach, all in perfect shape?' A touch more useful than my husband's reaction. You have to accept your body. Everybody is not a supermodel. Everybody is not the same shape. Just as you accept your face as unique, you must accept your body as unique.

Society conditions us to accept our face as unique. But when it comes to the body there is the perfect figure, an unattainable, unrealistic body stereotype that is ingrained into us by a host of media. This is not some vague ideal but is made up of specific measurements down to the last inch. The legendary 36-24-36. A big beauty multinational recently made a dent in this department by showcasing real curves and real women.

But we still need to learn to celebrate and accept our individual shapes. This does not give you a licence to be 100 kg. It means that after giving your body the healthiest helping hand you can, you have to accept what you were given. This is hard. In my head I still see myself as a fat person. I am working through this.

Thin pink

All my life I have been made to control my eating habits, and now everybody is forcing me to eat proper meals and stop losing weight. Quite a role reversal. Everyone from my mother to my family doctor keeps telling me, 'Ek baar muh utar gaya toh phir vapis nahin ata. You are at that crucial age of deterioration and you should not overdo it.' Once you lose too much weight too quickly or at a late stage in life, you lose the shape and glow of your face and it's gone for ever. It can't come back. Either way, I had all my tests done and the doctors said I am in the pink of health!

Faternally yours

For many years, the most important relationships in my life were dominated by my weight. Especially my relationship with my mother. She was the one who always pointed out the obvious, the glaring obesity. She was instrumental in finding me the next big thing as far as dieting and losing weight went.

Even when I was getting married, my mother was handing out weight wisdom. She told my husband, 'I have given her to you thin and beautiful. Now you make sure she stays that way. I officially resign.' She held back for a few years before she decided that she was not happy with his efforts. She worried about my weight affecting my marriage. She said, 'If you keep going this way he may still love you but he won't be attracted to you any more. You must keep yourself looking good for each other.' This and other such advice were not taken well and kept our relationship very volatile. Now that the kilos have gone, our relationship is still volatile but the tension point is not my weight.

Too sexy for my husband!

My husband relished the new me. When we had our ten-year anniversary party, he called it my relaunch party. But for him the real high was when we returned to the pendo wedding circuit in UK after ten years. We had not attended a single wedding on his side of the family because I was tired of fielding the 'I am not pregnant, and no I don't have a thyroid problem' questions from over-inquisitive badi buas.

I was at my sexiest best in a corset blouse and lehenga, dancing the gidda in a rented hall in Birmingham. My husband was talking to his uncle, the father of the groom. This was how their conversation went. It's written in Punjabi to retain the original flavour.

Uncle: Kiddan Raj, seeing you after long. *(How are you?)*
Husband: Changa. Congratulations. *(Good.)*
Uncle: Tu kalla aya hai? *(You have come alone?)*
Husband: Nahin toh, oh meri voti dance kardi pai hai.
(No, there is my wife dancing on the floor.)

Uncle: Haan haan, accha hai nayi voti le aya aur meno dasaya bhi nahin. Wah bhai wah, eh chald peya hai dilli vich. (*Ya, nice new wife you got. You did not even tell us. So this is what has been cooking in Delhi.*)

Husband: Nahin nahin. Mein toh... (*No, no, I am...*)

Uncle: Menu vyaa ch vi nahin sadya. Bhull gya, hain? (*You did not even call me for the wedding. Forgot about me, huh!*)

Husband: Oh nahin uncle. Eh tan ohi voti hai. Eh tan Kalli hi hai. (*No no. She is the same wife. That's Kalli.*)

Uncle: Good one, par eh oh nahin ho sakdi. Tu mazak kar raya hain. Mein enni nahin peeti!

(*No it can't be her. You are pulling my leg. I have not had that much to drink*)

Husband: Nahin nahin, ohi hai. (*No, no, it's her only.*)

Uncle: Sachhi? Par oh tan enni moti si. Tu sure hai?

(*Really? But she was so fat. Are you sure?*)

(Husband beaming and shaking his head.)

Relationshapes

Relationships have changed with my shape. My friends find the new me happier, calmer and more positive. They like the explosion of energy over the lump of lard. At work, my team is more confident of my abilities and business partners are more helpful. Even strangers' reactions towards me have changed. I find I can make a positive impression without even opening my mouth. Salesman are nicer, the maitre d' always find me a table and the social butterflies air kiss with more sincerity, though behind my back they continue to say things like, 'She is looking so good she must be having an affair.' Being leaner has made my life much rounder.

THINTERVENTION

The people closest to you can see what you are doing to yourself and they can't let you self-destruct or, in this case, over-construct. Nobody likes to be told they are fat, and when the nobody is an aggressive gorilla, people tend to shy away.

So, what do you do if the person you love is dangerously fat? It could be your friend, significant other, parent or, worse, your child. It's a tough one. Snide remarks and harsh words don't work. It just makes them feel depressed and eat more, particularly if you make the remarks in front of a room full of people. It has to be timed right.

What is the right timing? Well there is never really a right time to tell someone they are fat. But it is certainly not when they are getting dressed to go out with friends, attend an important meeting or on a date. This is soul destroying. It's not when they are about to indulge on their favourite dish. Because they are in the complete opposite frame of mind and the next bite will be you. One meal is not going to make a difference. Let them eat it. It's not when they are having a breakdown about being fat. That's when you need to be empathetic and come up with solutions and ideas on how you can support them.

Find the right window. Perhaps when you're having breakfast on a lazy weekend or in the evening when you are couching in front of the TV or when you're on a long drive. And always do it in private, as a one on one.

List out the things they can't do being fat. Saying 'You will have health problems' makes no difference. Make it tangible. Suggest specific solutions and plans. The name of a dietician, the number of a trainer, the timings of a class. In most cases, the fat person simply does not know how to solve the problem. Offer to walk the road with them by sacrificing dessert, or go to the gym with them, or give up partying for a while. He doesn't need to be told he is drowning; you need to throw him a lifejacket.

And remember, eventually, it has to come from within. For most fatties, it is one heartbreaking incident, like being rejected by prospective in-laws, breaking a chair at a restaurant, not getting the seat belt around the tummy on a plane, being asked if they are pregnant, seeing a photo of themselves, getting stuck in a dress in a fitting room… Be there for them when it happens, with a lot of love, compassion and a plan that does not involve chocolate.

SIR, THERE IS A FRY ON YOUR PLATE

Life must go on and you will go out for meals, so here are some of my favourite restaurant tricks:

- Always tell them to take away the bread basket and butter. Nobody on the table needs it. It ruins the appetite anyway.
- Ask for a low-calorie option. Restaurants are more often than not willing to accommodate with oil-free dressings and oil-free preparations.
- Soup is a low-calorie option only when it is not cooked in cream. Also, soup at night leads to water retention.
- Caesar's salad is not a light option, it is loaded with high-fat dressing, fried croutons and fatty bacon. It is better to order a green salad and always go for a balsamic dressing.
- Ask the waiter to replace the fries with something else or leave that space in the plate empty. Do not let the fries come to the table. It is very difficult not to have one. And then it is difficult to have just the one. Do not go down this oily slope.
- Never order a cappuccino at the end of a meal as compensation for not ordering dessert. The full-fat milk probably has more calories than a low-calorie dessert.

- Never eat at a buffet.
- Always strain out visible cream, butter and fat.
- Don't eat Indian food out. Indian food from restaurants is heavy and delicious and should not be eaten. It is loaded with ghee, butter, cream. Stick to Indian food at home. And if you must eat Indian out, stick to kebabs and the tandoor. No dal and curries, please.
- Two things can be eaten only once a year. Fries and jalebis. Choose your days well.
- Don't eat kiddie food. Ever. Smileys, chicken nuggets, coloured sugar-icing cookies are loaded with uncountable calories. I am not sure why we give them to our kids.
- Remember that going out and celebrating is about being out with family and friends, and not about the food.

Buffet

- Buffets are very tempting. You get to eat all the courses, something you may not do if you are ordering.
- In a buffet you will load your plate at least three times. Salad, mains and dessert. A minimum of three plates is not a good start.
- You end up eating more than you would if you were choosing and ordering. You would never eat three desserts if you were ordering from the menu.
- If something doesn't taste good you just change plates and continue eating.
- You always think you need to do justice to the buffet. You take more than you want because you have already paid for it and end up eating more than you need to.
- There is no portion control. If you like something, you can go back for more and more.
- Stick to à la carte. You have to stick to a portion, a choice, and probably a course.

Not Guilty

These are dishes that you can indulge in when out, which are instinctively low in calories and high in taste.

Delhi Favourites

Thai chicken / Vegetable Krapow served with brown rice	*360, Oberoi*
Plain dosa (no oil) with sambar and no coconut chutney	*Sagar Ratna*
Low-fat skinny mocha	*Barista*
Sugar-free mojito	*Magique*
Edamame beans and black cod	*ai*
Koli wada	*Swagat*
Raspberry and banana frozen yogurt	*Big Chill Café*
Beckti maacher paturi	*Oh! Calcutta*
Scrambled egg whites with brown bread	*Chokola*
Granola chunks	*Smokehouse Deli*

Mumbai Favourites

Home-made sugarfree ice-cream flavour or sorbet	*Indigo Deli*
Citrus and rocket salad	*Pali Village Café*
Baked rawas and vegetables	*Moshe's*
Hyderabadi pomfret	*Trishna*
Black pepper lobster	*Thai Pavilion*
Agadashi tofu	*San-Qi*
Balinese claypot of zucchini, babycorn and broccoli	*Joss*

Singaporean chilli crab	*Ling's Pavilion*
Gujarati thali	*Soma Babulnath*
Masala pomfret	*Mahesh Lunch Home*
Weekly spa lunch	*Blu*

Kolkata Favourites

Steamed and stewed rice	*Kim Fa*
Kebab roll with roti	*Nizam's*
Chelo kebab	*Peter Cat*
Hummus sandwich	*Picadilly*
Paper sada dosa	*Jyoti Vihar*
Lebanese wrap	*Café Mocha*
Steamed momos	*Humro Momo*
Beckti paturi	*Kewpies*
Thin crust pizza with grilled garden vegetables	*Spaghetti Kitchen*
Roasted Mediterranean vegetables platter	*La Rotisserie, Oberoi*
Low-fat apple pie	*Café Mocha*

Golden Calories

I know foodies whose ultimate indulgence is to read recipe books in bed so that they can have sweet dreams. It's like food porn. This list falls in that category. They are very, very special-occasion indulgences. The calories are worth their weight in gold. This is the stuff I fantasize about. Mostly!

Golden Calories

Millefeuille at the Oberoi patisserie
Chocolate ganache at Magique
Mississippi mud pie at Big Chill Café
Flourless chocolate cake at Smokehouse Deli
Chiang Mai train station noodles at Mamagoto
Yam Phak Krob Rumait at Ego Thai
Date pancakes at House of Ming, Taj Palace Hotel
Chocolate soufflé at Diva
Camembert soufflé at Orient Express
Parmesan cheese and syruped figs at La Piazza
Hot chocolate fudge sundae at Nirula's
Chocolate macaroons and almond croissants at L'Opera (anything at L'Opera, even the paper napkin!)

My Favourite Fillers

Masala chai with Stevicol (a natural low-calorie sweetener made from the Stevia herb)

Popcorn without butter

Makhana (lotus seeds)

Channa chaat

Fruit

Yoghurt with tarka

Sweet fruit with chat masala

Black coffee with skimmed milk

Herbal tea

Water

WE ARE GOING ON A HOLYDAY

You cannot diet on holiday. You can try and follow healthy guidelines. But, by definition, a holiday means letting loose, indulging, spoiling yourself, doing the things you normally would not do.

Even now I make promises to myself regularly before I go on holiday. I am going to diet on this holiday and be very good because I have no stress. I don't have to eat fatty work lunches or eat to deal with stress. I will work out all day. I will eat only healthy and on time because I can control my timings. I have found that these are silly ideas and put pressure on me for no reason. But I still do them; awareness doesn't always lead to change in behaviour.

You can read my holiday diaries. They are shocking. I have included them because I don't want you to beat yourself up about not following the rules on holiday. Don't set yourself up for disaster. Set a reasonable target for the holiday. Mine is that I will not put on weight on my holiday. And I will get back on the plan the minute the holiday is over.

Holiday Diary: Goa

9:00 a.m. At the hotel gym. Workout for 25 minutes on cross-trainer to burn 250. *(This is at a hotel I have stayed at three times before this and did not even know there was a gym. Good progress.)*
Yoga class on the beach
My own 100 surya namaskars in 14 minutes
Swim 6 lengths of the giant pool

My commitment to exercise was a pleasant surprise to me.

11:00 a.m. Buffet breakfast (*I broke my golden rule of not eating from the buffet*)

Birchermuesli blended with apples, yoghurt and possibly cream with a topping of crunchy muesli and raisins

Two butter croissants further toasted for extra crispiness with slices of Edam cheese and sour cream and capers

Sugar and cinnamon doughnut

Cappuccino

Work for a couple of hours.

1.45 p.m. Open-air pedicure with girlfriend. One hour of bliss.

3.30 p.m. Chilli cheese toast

Penne tossed in extra virgin olive oil, burnt garlic, red chilli flakes and vegetables topped with parmesan

Mixed green salad

Ice-cream sundae layered with mixed berry compote and peaches

Mojitos

5.30 p.m. Meditation by the beach

6.15 p.m. Sunset swim in the sea

7.30 p.m. Clear the mind with some deep breathing and meditation by the sea

9.00 p.m. No dinner plan so I order cold coffee. Cold coffee is without ice-cream but with sugar and accompanied by delicious freshly-baked all butter cookies.

9.20 p.m. No-dinner resolve broken. Order bruschetta, eat half. Then start gorging on chicken reshmi kebab and paneer tikka with crispy nan and kali dal.

11.00 p.m. Movie in hotel theatre with butter popcorn

Holiday Diary: Manali

7:00 a.m. Yoga class

Find and join an advanced yoga class for one-and-a-half hours a day. Wake up at seven, get out of my cosy razai, get into my workout gear, trudge up a mini mountain in the pouring rain. It is Bihar school of yoga and it involves ropes. I do a headstand on ropes. Big high.

9:00 a.m. Breakfast

Woody's roasted muesli with figs, nuts and dried fruit with bananas and milk

Overstuffed omelet with buttered toast

Many cups of tea

1:00 p.m. Picnic lunch (provided by Italian chef)

Pasta with chicken, pepper and olive oil

Angel hair spaghetti with cherry tomato and parmesan

Roast chicken

Extra buttery quiche

Green salad with olives

Walnut and caramel pie

White wine

2:00 p.m. Comatose sleep under apple tree surrounded by mountains to the sound of the stream.

4:00 p.m. Walk on the dry river bed, uphill, negotiating river rocks and stones.

Tea from a thermos and digestive biscuits

6:00 p.m. One hour walk to the Mall road

Blueberry cheesecake and cappuccino

Drive back to the house.

9:00 p.m. Dinner

Meat curry with potatoes and white rice and spring onions

Jam tart made in buttery pastry and Kisan strawberry jam

Some reasonable holiday rules

Don't drink during the day just because you are on holiday. Do it when you really want to. Night drinking is okay but day drinking can easily be avoided.

Include some kind of activity, exercise or otherwise. Don't take the golf cart in the resort. Volunteer to fetch the forgotten thing from the room. Carry the shopping bags. Use the stairs. Avoid all-day-in-bed holidays. Work on building that appetite.

Get back on your diet plan from the last meal of the holiday. Do not wait till you are back home. Start compensating not from tomorrow, but from a happy place, from the last meal of your holiday. This is not easy but it is the most effective trick.

Wear a well-fitted set of clothes. Comfortable but with little room to grow. Wear the same clothes on the way back. Somewhere in the back of your mind, you will know that at the end of the holiday you still need to fit into the same pair of jeans you came in.

Before you go on holiday, find that one high-calorie food you are likely to consume a lot of during the holiday and vow to give it up. Just that one food. On a recent trip to Manali, I gave up chocolate. I knew the cold weather and the warm fire would tempt me to eat industrial quantities of chocolate. I vowed not to touch chocolate. This helps because your body feels like it is giving up only one thing. It's not major denial so you accept it, even on holiday.

When on holiday, focus on exercise rather than denying yourself food.

If you are on a buffet package, try and eat only one buffet a day.

AND SHE DIETED HAPPILY EVER AFTER

The book launch is freaking me out. Who is going to buy a diet book written by a fatty? I am desperate to get back on track but the book deadlines are stressing me out. All the late-night editing means no sleep and midnight fridge raids. Luckily, since the fridge is destocked (I do practise what I preach), I don't come back with much. But there are sweeties from my kids' birthday party loot bags.

My friends have been telling me that if I keep going at this rate, by the time we launch the book I will be so fat I will have to use a life-size thin cutout in place of myself.

I have been planning a new diet every day for the last ten days. I start with one diet and end with another. The dangers of too much knowledge. What weight am I going to be when you see me next? I don't know. I may not be as thin as I would like to be but I will surely be on the next diet that will get me there. And *that's* the secret to being thin. Anyone who is working it, is working on it.

Sssssh! New diet in progress...

THANK YOU

Thank you, Babies
For demanding so much more that I had to become less. For encouraging me to 'colour' my book, otherwise people would not buy it and they would remain motu!

Thank you, Husband
For standing by me and always being so adoring even when I was 100 kg. But next time you love me so much that I can't see what I have become, I will squash you with all my newly gained kilos!

Thank you, Mother
For being my first self-appointed dietician. For coming up with the most innovative carrots to convince me to live on celery. And for coming up with the most cutting dietary advice: 'Nobody wants a fat wife.' I am glad to have retired you from your thankless job.

Thank you, Sister
For graciously sharing your position as the beautiful and glamorous sibling. For always telling it like it is. And for marrying the Frenchman.

Thank you, Friends
For banishing the word 'tuntun' from your vocabulary, for putting up with my Ma Kali avatar and for being my non-paid board of advisors and editors.

To all my dieticians and trainers: I hate you like I love you!
For putting your all into my transformation. In particular, Dr Calm, DD and Hotshot, you know who you are, this book, this me, would not have been possible without you. Eternal gratitude.

Connect with me

Write to me @ Kalli@theserialdieter.com

Visit my website: www.theserialdieter.com

Twitter: www.twitter.com/theserialdieter

Facebook: www.facebook.com/theserialdieter

To subscribe to my daily weight wisdom on your
mobile phone sms SUB DIET to 52424.
(Only for Airtel subscribers)

For a one-time shot of weight wisdom on your
mobile phone sms DIET to 52424.
(Available to all mobile subscribers)